Chin Hairs & Back Fat

Somewhere Between Tweezers, Yoga Pants & a Box of Wine

VIKKI CLAFLIN

Mill Park Publishing
www.MillParkPublishing.com

FIRST EDITION, FEBRUARY 2017

Published in the United States by Mill Park Publishing 2017

Library of Congress has cataloged this edition as follows:
Claflin, Vikki 1956, September 11 – Chin Hairs & Back Fat: Somewhere Between Tweezers, Yoga Pants & a Box of Wine/by Vikki Claflin – 1st U.S. edition.

PRINT ISBN: 978-0-9883-9808-5
EBOOK ISBN: 978-0-9883-9809-2

Book cover by Michele Fairbanks, Fresh Design
Edited by Kathryn F. Galán

Disclaimer of Liability
The author and/or editor shall have neither liability nor responsibility to any person or entity with respect to any loss or damage caused or alleged to be caused directly or indirectly by the information contained in this book.

Praise For CHIN HAIRS & BACK FAT

"A chuckle/snort/laugh-out-loud book about life in the AARP lane. Vikki Claflin is a charming storyteller and has a sense of humor that will make you love her, crinkles and all."
~ Anne Bardsley, *How I Earned My Wrinkles*

"Another hilariously funny smash hit. The title grabs you right in the midlife section! It flows so effortlessly, you feel you're having a cocktail with your best friend and you don't want it to end."
~ Ellen Dolgen, *Menopause Mondays: The Girlfriends' Guide to Surviving & Thriving During Perimenopause and Menopause*

"Vikki Claflin has a superpower, and it's her uncanny ability to make the aging crap we're all dealing with laugh-out-loud funny. She's the girlfriend who always knows just what to say—and, most importantly, when to pour the wine. You'll laugh your ass off—which, at this age, can be a good thing, in more ways than one."
~ Roxanne Jones, boomerhaiku.com

"Vikki Claflin does it again. Channeling her inner-Erma Bombeck, she tells it like it is, makes it real, and lets us know what's what … all with humor and love. If you haven't read her previous books and don't follow her blog, shame on you! This book is a good place to start!"
~ Paul Brads, rednecklatte.com.

"From body hair to relationships, from life clutter to mental health, Vikki Claflin shows comedic mercy where the calendar refuses to. *Chin Hairs & Back Fat* stirs up the perfect snarky cocktail for all 50-plus vixens and those who have to live with us."

Becky Blades, *Do Your Laundry or You'll Die Alone*

"Just reading the title clued me in to hold on and get ready to laugh—and who couldn't use a good laugh these days!? This latest book is fun to read, witty, and wise. Congrats, Vikki! You knocked another one outta the ballpark!"

~ Lynne Cobb, contributor, *Feisty After 45*

"In a world full of messages telling us that getting older must be resisted with every ounce of cream, medical procedure, and act of denial a woman can muster, Claflin offers refreshingly funny permission to embrace the changes as they come. You'll find this to be The Guide to being a badass, make-no-excuses, confident woman!"

~ Tara Reed, Caregiver Coach, pivottohappy.com

"Vikki Claflin has done it again with her latest collection of witty tales from midlife and beyond. Claflin is the BFF we all wish we had because she tells it like it is and leaves us laughing until our bellies hurt. Grab a glass of wine and settle in for an enjoyable read. You won't be able to put this one down."

~ Marcia Kester Doyle, *Who Stole my Spandex?*

"She did it again! Vikki Claflin's latest is a laugh-out-loud, snort-soda (*ok, wine*)-up-your-nose read. "Maybe 60 is finally time to embrace the journey," she says, and proceeds to do just that with hysterical listicles and hilarious, heartfelt advice. Irreverent, funny, and frank, Vikki writes like Erma Bombeck—with a razor-sharp edge."

~ Liane Kupferberg Carter, *Ketchup Is My Favorite Vegetable:*
A Family Grows Up With Autism

"I've never met her in person, but I'm pretty sure Claflin and I could do some serious damage at a wine bar. Nothing's sacred, she doesn't take herself too seriously, and she has a remarkable tendency to tell it like it is. My kind of woman.

~ AK Turner, *Vagabonding with Kids*

"Vikki Claflin meets the advancement of the clock with humor, hilarities, and enough wisdom to make me look forward to aging, versus dreading it like the death march through a dry desolate hell I've always assumed it would be. From the hilarious truths about aging, to tips and tricks for our beleaguered husbands, this book will have you laughing and wanting more."

~ Alyson Herzig, *Surviving Mental Illness Through Humor*

"Reality is never easier to digest than when served with side of humor! I love Ms. Claflin's take on life and aging. She's as honest as it gets, but in a way that leaves you nodding enthusiastically amid fits of giggles. My chin hairs give this book five stars!"

~ Beth Teliho, *Order of Seven*

"The future is indeed bright, if a bit hairy and jiggly. Vikki Claflin embraces aging with humor and grace that is neither age nor gender specific. Readers of all ages will delight in Claflin's stories on friendship, love, beauty, and family. Women (and married men) will connect and take comfort in these touching and hilarious truths from someone who's been there, done that, and tells all."

~ Kathryn Mayer, Writer, Humorist, kathrynmayer.com

"Vikki Claflin writes about aging with humor and heart. When you finish this book, you'll want to give her a big hug and say 'Thank you, thank you,' for making you realize you are not alone. And that aging really is a state of mind."

~ Janie Emaus, janieemaus.com

"When I was a kid, 'A' was not the highest mark one could achieve in school. 'H' was. I'm giving Vikki Claflin both. 'H' for Hilarious and at times, Hysterical; 'A' for Attitude. Only Attitude will get you through the wonder years, when you wonder where your mind, your figure, your teeth and your sex-appeal went. If you haven't read Vikki Claflin, read this book!"
~ Diane Tolley, *Daughter of Ishmael*

"Hey, you. Yeah, you! You of the youthful outlook, the unhindered sense of style, the unapologetic free-thinker who's *finally* comfortable in your own skin, have I got a book for you! Humorist Vikki Claflin is back, with a hilarious and relatable take on midlife. Written with Claflin's trademark wit and conversational style, you'll feel like you're having cocktails with your best friend, sharing life's most head-scratchy, amusing moments and coming away feeling better for it."
~ Linda Roy, contributor, *I Still Just Want to Pee Alone*

"Vikki Claflin writes about aging with humor and heart. When you finish this book, you'll want to give her a big hug and say 'Thank you, thank you,' for making you realize you are not alone. And that aging really is a state of mind."
~ Janie Emaus, janieemaus.com

"There is humor and liberation in the truths about aging and being married, and Vikki Claflin nails them in her newest book. Every hubby and wife should buy this book, read it, and give it to their spouse! It will 'bring in a certain peace … a letting go of the anxieties and limited perspectives of youth.' Also, lots of belly laughs!"
~ Lisa Nolan, *Motherhood May Cause Drowsiness:*
Stories from the Trenches.

To Hubs
Seventeen years and still
living the dream

To Joella -
Because we all
need just a little
crazy in our lives! ☺

Table of Contents

A Gift for You!

SIGN UP for my mailing list to get updates on book releases, cover reveals, and other fun stuff, and never miss a post!

As a Thank You, I'll send you my *Ninja Closet Cleaning Course (What to Toss, What to Keep)*, and show you how to love your clothes again! It's one of my most-requested articles, and it's reserved only for subscribers.

Simply go to http://laugh-lines.net/, enter your name and email address, then click "DOWNLOAD NOW" for instant access.

It's fun, and it's FREE!

(I'll never share your name or email address, nor will I spam you.)

"In old age, you must put
up with the face,
the friends, the health,
and the children you have
earned."

~ Judith Viorst

I'm 60. How the Hell Did That Happen?

THIS YEAR, I'm turning sixty. 6-0. As in "years old."

How is this possible? Yesterday, I swear I was forty. I'll always be forty. I *liked* forty. But I woke up this morning and I'm twenty (count 'em... *twenty*) years older than I feel. That's a whole lifetime for a college student. So I'm an entire lifetime older than the average undergraduate. Awesome.

Turning twenty was fun. You're officially an adult but you're young enough to have your mistakes forgiven, because you're still a puppy to the rest of the world. Thirty was great. You're more sophisticated now and have started making "life decisions." Marriage? Kids? A mortgage? A beagle or a dachshund? And forty is *sexy*. You're a woman, not a girl. You're *interesting*. You have things to say, and people actually want to hear them. At fifty, you've run smack into midlife. I'll admit: fifty was a little tough for me. All that push to get an AARP card, remembering to ask for the Honor Menu at every restaurant, and deciding whether or not to go gray, now that you're a "senior."

Sixty leaves me somewhat stymied. I have no precise words to express exactly how I feel about it. It's clearly not "middle age" (unless we're planning to live to be 120). We've been seniors for ten years already. So what are we now?

I recently attended my forty-second high school reunion. It was a wonderful evening of wine and laughter, with much to-do about getting older. Many of us expressed the same observation: everybody looked great but somehow *older* than we remembered them. Then, when we saw the photos on Facebook the next day, we noticed we all look exactly the same age as everyone else. Boom.

The publishing world is full of books, articles, and websites about the frustrations and seemingly inevitable downfalls of aging. Whether we see it from a humorous perspective or as something to approach from a fetal position on the bed, sobbing into an oversize decanter of cabernet, there's nary a woman alive who can't recount tales of aging woes.

By sixty, our body parts have shifted downward, our skin has lost elasticity, we still experience occasional menopausal flashbacks that make us human space heaters, and our weight has moved into our bellies and hips like squatters on the Back 40 of the Ponderosa.

But I've decided that I'm giving myself a birthday present this year. I'm giving myself a break about the aging thing. Yes, I'm aware that my boobs haven't been within howdy-neighbor proximity of my clavicles for at least two decades and that my butt jiggles like a Jell-O mold, even when I'm standing still. But maybe sixty is finally time to embrace the journey. Youth may come with smooth skin and perky behinds, but often in exchange for angst and uncertainty. (Honestly, would you *be* twenty-five again??) Middle age (and beyond) brings with it a certain peace. A letting go of the anxieties and often limited perspectives of youth. It's *liberating*.

And so, for my birthday, to balance the scales of publishing, I've decided to write down my **Most Fabulous Things About Turning Sixty**.

1. **We've learned to accept our bodies**. Gone are the days of puking, pills, eating nothing but grapefruit and chewing gum, full-body Spanx under everything, and workouts that leave us shaky and exhausted instead of energized, as we futilely try to beat our ancestral gene pool into submission and create a body we were never designed to have. I'm short and curvy, and I've given birth. (Although my son is now twenty-seven and says I really must stop blaming my jelly belly on him. Ungrateful brat).

2. **The world is less black and white**. We're less quick to judge. By now, we know that every story has three sides: yours, mine, and what really happened. When we hear that Aunt Bebe ran off with Uncle Stu's Krav Maga instructor, we're less likely to assume Aunt Bebe is simply a tramp who likes martial arts and more likely to reply, "There are probably pieces of this story we don't know."

3. **We get to wear whatever we want**. At this age, fashion, which tends to target the young and the anorexic, is more about what we know works for *us* than what's on Project Runway. Love leather moto jackets? We wear ours with everything we own. Hate trendy, low-rise jeans that give you Texas-size muffin top? We get to skip this one.

4. **There's less drama**. After six decades, we begin to realize that not *everything* is worth fighting over. As my grandma used to say, "In fifty years, we'll all be dead and none of this will matter."

5. **We get grandchildren**. We've had the responsibility of raising tiny humans into socially acceptable adults. Now we get to simply love the crap out of our offspring's mini-

mes, with our primary role being somewhere between Obi Wan Kenobi and Santa Claus.

6. **We learn to cherish our girlfriends**. We've attended Sally's four weddings, got Missy through three stints in rehab, and lived through Susie's douchy husband's affair. We've supported Jenny's new career as a nude art model, bailed Karen's son out of jail (again), and cried together when Linda got cancer. We have *history*.

7. **Our marriages are stronger**. There's no way two people can spend several decades together and have every day be a lust-filled day of mutual wonder and adoration. Not. Possible. We've had rough times, disappointments, and days when we'd unhesitatingly sell each other for a frosted margarita from the local taco wagon. But we're still together. It's *that* kind of love.

8. **We laugh more**. We see the silliness in things more easily. We're not as easily offended. Simply put, we've lightened up.

9. **We've discovered new passions**. Boomers are being called "The Reinvented Generation." We're going back to school, learning new languages, traveling to new places, running marathons, and writing novels. We're not retiring. We're living longer than ever, and we're doing it in a red convertible.

So, as I kiss my fifties goodbye and face a new decade, I feel… well… *good*. In fact, I feel better than good. I feel like getting out there and kicking some jiggly ass.

""*Women have more imagination than men. They need it to tell us how wonderful we are.*"

~ Arnold H. Glasow

The Day Hubs Began to Understand Women

HUBS HAS always been super fit. He's a natural athlete who excels at everything he tries (yeah, like *that's* never annoying), and he's been in construction for thirty years, so he has no need for pedestrian things like treadmills and rowing machines at home. For years, he's been able to buy jeans simply by size. Dressing rooms are an enigma to this man.

"Why do people need to try these on?" he asks, looks slightly confused. "There's a size label right on the back."

I grit my teeth and try to explain that, unlike most *women*, men have no need to haul fourteen pairs in twelve different fits and seven brands into a stuffy dressing room, jump up and down to hike them up, and hate them all, until we finally give up, sweaty and defeated, leaving the entire pile in a twisted heap on the floor as we exit the store in our yoga pants, empty-handed, and do the walk of shame to the nearest wine bar. Well, maybe not *all* women. Okay, maybe just me.

But, over the last few years, Hubs has gotten, well… older. Like many men, he's finding that middle age, while bringing a certain level of wisdom and inner peace, can also come with physical changes they don't always anticipate or prepare for.

Hubs just assumed that he'd always look like he did in college. All buffed, defined, and hot.

Women know better. Menopause hits us like a speeding Mac truck, letting us know in no uncertain terms that we are no longer young. We're fully aware that we will forever battle with butts and boobs heading south with the determination of migrating geese in the winter. We're prepared for the sudden appearance of back fat and chin hair. We sigh over the inevitable weight gain and regularly inspect the backs of our thighs like zealous Pinkerton agents, pinching for fat clumps we know everybody else can see, even if we can't.

Women prepare for midlife in a number of ways. Almost every woman I know over forty has a minimum of two sizes in her closet: her "skinny clothes" and her "fat clothes." Some women have three or four size options. In the same closet. Choices on any given day depend on our weight, our mood, and our confidence levels.

Hubs can get dressed in a blackout. He reaches into his closet, grabs something that feels like jeans, tosses on a T-shirt and his one pair of sneakers, and he's good to go. No lighting necessary. And not even a glance in a mirror on his way out. (But I'm not jealous. Really, I'm not.) However, this last year, he had a little taste of "life on the other side."

One morning, he sat down at breakfast and announced we were going shopping. It seemed that all his jeans were too tight.

"Are you using a different laundry soap?" he asked, looking befuddled when his couldn't button his beloved 501s.

"It's not the soap, sweetie," I replied. "You need a 36."

"How is that *possible*?" he stuttered. "I wear a 34."

"No," I said, "you *wore* a 34. You *wear* a 36."

"Well," he said with a sigh, "this just sucks." He wasn't happy about it, and neither of us mentioned it again. Until the 36s didn't fit.

We were shopping for some slacks for an upcoming event, and the sales guy looked at Hubs and smiled, "So, sir, a 38 pant?"

Oh, crap.

Hubs looked horrified, grabbed me by the arm, and hauled me into the dressing room. "*A 38 pant*?" he whispered, "Is he *kidding* me??"

"Well, honey…" I scrambled for an answer that wouldn't hurt his feelings but was still grounded in reality. (He *had* been hitting the late-night Ben & Jerry's pretty hard that winter…) "It's not about *you*. Lots of clothes are made in Taiwan now. The fit models are tiny little people, so *their* 38 and *our* 38 can be very different. Plus, there's a lot of play in seam allowances. You need to just ignore the size label and go for the fit." (Seriously, by now I was starting to babble.)

"So do *you* think I'm fat??" he insisted.

"No!" I said. "You've just put on a little weight because you're less active and a little older. Nothing to worry about."

"Well," he harrumphed, "as long as you don't think I'm *fat*."

"Absolutely not," I reassured him as best I could, "*Honest*."

Eventually, Hubs got busy again at work and his weight returned to a more normal range. Then recently, as we were weeding out our closets, he found the pants he'd bought on that fateful day. He held them up, pulled them wide, and announced, "Look at these! Wow, these fit me last year."

"Uh huh," I replied, trying quickly to change the subject because I knew where it was going.

He looked over me, frowning. "You said I wasn't fat. These are for a fat person. I was fat, wasn't I?"

"Well, *fat* is a subjective term," I stammered.

"And what was all that crap about 'tiny Taiwanese people?'" he demanded. "It doesn't matter if *they're* tiny. They were making clothes for big ol' Americans, in a size 38, which I *wore*. And that seam allowance thing?? I *believed* you."

I frantically tried to defend myself. "Well, what was I supposed to say?"

"I asked you if I was fat, and you said *no*," he accused. "Why didn't you *tell* me??"

"Because you *never* tell a fat person they're fat," I replied. "Every woman knows that. That's just *mean*. But now that you're not fat anymore, I can tell you. Holy crap, you were a chunky monkey."

"You have no credibility anymore," he grumbled. "But should I save these, just in case I ever get 'not fat' again?"

"Can't hurt." I smiled. "You can just put them in the bottom drawer with mine."

Fat pants. Apparently they're not just for women anymore.

"Today is Valentine's Day.
Or, as men like to call it,
Extortion Day"

~ Jay Leno

You Shouldn't Have.
Really, You Shouldn't
The Husband's Guide to Valentine's Day

THE CHRISTMAS season is finally over, with barely a chance to take a breath before retailers begin frantically loading their shelves with Valentine's Day cards, gifts, and ads extolling the romantic features of wind-up, plastic teddy bears. Many women, like me, love Valentine's Day. It's all about romance, falling in love, and tiny cherubs flying around in the clouds, shooting tiny arrows through the hearts of mortals to signal the successful pairing of potential soul mates.

For men, Valentine's Day is often a bit more *practical*. It's the universe's way of giving you a Do-Over day. Twenty-four hours to give her the romantic gift you *didn't* get her for Christmas. Yes, in fact, she did need new brake pads for her car, but, as a Christmas gift, it lacked a certain level of intimacy. Okay, it sucked.

Any gift to your wife should be personal and thoughtful. But on Valentine's Day, she wants to feel especially loved, cherished, and important to you. She wants bragging rights with her girlfriends, so they know what a lucky woman she is to be

You Shouldn't Have. Really, You Shouldn't.

15

married to a sweetheart like you. You're right, it can be a lot of pressure for a man.

To help you out and ensure that you're still happily married on February *15th*, here's a list of bad Valentine's Day gifts received by women from their misguided, but well-intended husbands. If you're considering any of these, be very careful (and include a really, *really* great card).

- ❖ **Cliche gifts**. Think generic flowers and heart-shaped boxes of candy. She hears, "Oh crap. It's Valentine's Day?? I guess I can stop on the way home and grab something from the display at Safeway." And if you want to give her flowers, get her favorite. (Hint: We don't all love red roses.) This is *not* the day for her to find out, after nine years, you don't know she loves purple Gerbera daisies.

- ❖ **Tacky lingerie**. This would be anything you bought at a store that also carries automotive accessories and children's craft products. Nylon panties adorned with badly stuck-on black lace, attached to a matching bra, are skeevy and say more about you than her. If you fantasize about cheap prostitutes, this isn't the time to bring her up to speed.

- ❖ **Cheap jewelry that makes no sense**. Necklaces with flimsy chains and pendants of plated dolphin tails when she's never expressed a love of the sea. Ditto ankle bracelets from Claire's, if she's forty-two.

- ❖ **Gag gifts**. Make light of your relationship on any other day of the year and you'll probably get a pass. On Valentine's Day, she may snuff you in your sleep. Toilet paper emblazoned with red hearts and "I love you all over" inscriptions on every sheet. Oversized, fleece pajama bags built for two. Juvenile couple's T-shirts (e.g., His: "I Heart Hooters." Hers: "Hi, I'm Hooters.")

❖ **Drugstore fragrances**. Especially if she wears Chanel, Armani, or another high-end scent. And don't even think about the lower-priced knock-offs that claim to smell "just like the original, for one-third the price." They don't. They smell like street hookers on parade.

❖ **A puppy**. *Seriously*? Unless she's expressed an unfulfilled desire for a pet, you've just handed her a fifteen-year project that eats, needs constant attention, will probably chew her favorite pair of expensive black boots, and may or may not know to do his business outside.

❖ **A personalized star on the Internet registry**. Stupidest. Gift. Ever. It's not like she can go there and stay for the weekend, or that she'll ever actually know which of the 700 gazillion stars in the sky is hers. This was *so* not invented by a woman.

❖ **Gift cards**. Even if you get the store right, you're saying, "I know where you shop, but I have no idea what you'd want." Really, dude? You've been married to her for thirteen years, you see her every day, and you can't visualize one thing she might like you to buy for her? If you're truly that unaware of her tastes, go to her favorite store and ask the saleswoman. And be nice. She can save your oblivious ass.

❖ **Stuffed animals**. Especially those holding tiny heart boxes of chocolate. What are we, like, twelve? And she knows you just grabbed it at Rite Aid while you were picking up your meds. It doesn't make her feel cherished when you only remembered Valentine's Day while refilling your prescription for irritable bowel syndrome.

❖ **Any gift that suggests she needs improvement**. This includes new scales, free weights, treadmills, memberships to Jenny Craig or Weight Watchers, or books

You Shouldn't Have. Really, You Shouldn't.

17

titled *How to Be a Better Lover in 14 Days*. Whether or not you think she *needs* these things is not the point. She just doesn't need them on Valentine's Day.

I know. By now, I've exhausted your original list and you're thinking, "So what *do* I get her??" It's easy.

A couple's massage at her favorite spa. A leisurely, romantic dinner at the restaurant of her choice. Lotion and powder in her signature fragrance. A bottle of wine she loves but won't buy because it's "too expensive." The newest book from her favorite author. Tickets to a play, opera, comedy club, or ballet that she wants to see. A pair of fabulous gloves to wear with her "she wears it every day" jacket. Anything that shows you've *listened* to her over the years. You've noticed her. *You love her.*

A friend of mine told me about a Valentine's Day when her Hubs brought home a half-dozen romantic comedies that he'd been steadfastly refusing to watch with her. He unplugged his phone and spent the entire day watching rom-coms with her, *without* falling asleep. He later claimed it was the best sex he'd ever had. Boom.

"Beauty has so many forms
I think the most beautiful thing
is confidence and loving
yourself."

~ Kiesza

11 Things Confident Women Do

(And You Can, Too)

AGING IN our society can be tough. Especially if you're a woman. With fourteen-year-old models on the cover of *Vogue*, it's generally well recognized that our culture is disinclined to promote confidence in women over fifty.

Beauty in America is largely defined by *youth*: firm thighs, perky (preferably large) breasts, toned underarms, and smooth skin from head to toe. If you're young with long blonde hair and legs like a giraffe, you don't even have to know the Queen's English. For those of us not genetically blessed to start with, by the time we get to fifty, sixty, or beyond, it can get harder and harder to feel good about ourselves or our bodies.

But every now and then, we come across a fifty-plus woman who seems to be genuinely confident about herself. She's often not even what we've been taught is the definition of "beautiful," yet she radiates a certain something that makes her seem so. Upon closer inspection, she's got lines around her eyes, her legs are short, her boobs have obviously tangled with gravity, and is that cellulite on her thighs?? How is it that she's got everyone talking about how gorgeous she is?

Glad you asked.

Personality studies have reported that one of the most important traits in confident women is they don't look to outside sources to validate their fabulousness. They instill it in themselves. They have lists of easy tips and habits that they're almost always delighted to share. They aren't threatened by the rest of us. The prevailing attitude is, "C'mon in. The water's fine." I love these women. Give these a try:

1. **Just once, get your photo taken by a Photoshop pro**. Photoshop can lighten, tighten, and reconfigure every part of your body. (Do you really think those fashion models look like that in real life?) It can smooth the skin, eliminate facial lines, narrow the waist, perk up your boobs, and even make your legs look longer. Put that photo up on Facebook. Use it as your profile picture on all of your social media sites. Send a framed copy to your mother, your best friend, and your ex (take *that*, jackass).

2. **Surround yourself with positive, happy people who love you and tell you how amazing you are**. "Oh, you shaved your head during that last stint in rehab? You look gorgeous!" "You're quitting your job at the law firm to build yurts? What a great idea!" These are the people who make us feel instantly better about ourselves. We *like* these people. Invite them over. A lot. And give them wine.

3. **Dump everyone else**. Critical, judgmental, snarky people who constantly belittle you or demean your achievements and generally make you feel like crap after five minutes in the same room together. It doesn't matter if you two were college roommates in 1980, or you were the maid of honor at her wedding twenty-four years ago, or even if you share DNA. "You're going to screw this up. You always do." "Aren't you a little old to take that risk?" "Oh, you self-published your book? Couldn't find a real publisher,

huh?" These kinds of comments can blast your confidence to smithereens because obviously you're stupid and your ideas are stupid, and you just need to sit in the corner with a pint of Ben & Jerry's until you get realistic about your shortcomings. Oh *hell* no. Get rid of these people. Do it today.

4. **Throw out your bathroom scale**. Starting every day by stepping on your scale, looking down, and announcing *"Yep, I'm still fat"* is virtually guaranteed to make you feel ugly or unworthy for the rest of the day. This one is so important, if you want to stop reading and go do it now, we'll wait.

5. **If you can't bring yourself to toss it, set it back three to five pounds**. Trust me, this works. In a couple of weeks, you'll forget that it's light, but you'll be five pounds nicer to yourself.

6. **Say something positive to yourself in the mirror every morning**. Positive self-talk or affirmations have been around for decades because *they work*. The brain believes what it's been told. Go goofy here. Nobody will hear it but you. *"Damn*, I'm sexy." "Good morning, gorgeous!" "I've got me a fabulous boo-tay!" Whatever makes you laugh. Do this for twenty-one straight days, and I promise you'll be rocking your rebel self all day long. (No weight loss or Botox required.)

7. **Cancel your subscriptions to magazines geared toward girls significantly younger than you**. You know, the ones that feature genetically anorexic, Photoshopped child models who've never reproduced or eaten a cheeseburger, modeling clothes we couldn't get into if we soaped ourselves up first. If we're going to compare ourselves to

other women, let's at least give ourselves a fighting chance by picking women in our own age bracket.

8. **Laugh**. As much as you can. You can't feel bad about yourself when you're laughing. It's *not possible*. Besides, you're a lot more fun to be around when you're happy, which attracts all of your positive, happy friends (see #2). So laugh. Do it often. And learn to laugh at yourself. You have the material you'll need.

9. **Stand up straight**. This is a small but empowering change you can make right now. Slouching pushes out the tummy, shortens our torso, and droops our boobs down closer to our navels. It says, "Don't notice me. Just pretend I'm not here." There's something about shoulders back, head up, and boobs forward that makes you feel (and look) like *"I got this."*

10. **Find the best candid picture of you ever taken**. Put it where you can see it regularly. Tape a copy to your bathroom mirror. That's how your positive, happy friends see you. To us, you're beautiful.

11. **Put it in perspective**. I've never heard anyone say at a funeral, "Beatrice was such a wonderful person, and we all loved her. But none of us could figure out why she couldn't bang off those last fifteen pounds." People. Don't. Care. If *you* care, do something about it. If you don't, don't. It truly only matters to you. The positive people in your life love you in any shape or form you come in, because you're... well, *you*.

"As for tweeting and texting:
impassioned discussions
don't work in abbreviated script
messages.
No relationship should begin or
end in 140 characters."

~ Mariella Frostrup

I Filed for Divorce.
Didn't You Get My Text?

CONDUCT ANY kind of survey, and you'd be hard pressed to find anyone who doesn't agree that social media has forever changed the way our society communicates.

Conversations that used to have to wait until we saw each other in person or when one of us got the message on our answering machine after we got home from work now take place instantly. We have Facebook, Twitter, Google+, Pinterest, and dozens of other social cyber groups that we can use to dazzle thousands of people we've never actually met with reports and photos of our exciting or perfect lives, or solicit (and receive) virtual group hugs because some disaster has befallen us.

In most cases, I love Facebook. Twitter has its purposes. And Pinterest can be downright addicting. The communication mode that continues to baffle me is texting.

It's not that I don't know how to do it (my then-ten-year-old taught me). Or that it's become the downfall of English grammar and punctuation (without question). Or even that I see people doing it at work, at restaurants, at movie theaters, and, stupidly, while driving (yep, people are still doing that). But I recently stood next to a couple texting each other while *in the same room.*

It was all I could do to not grab the guy and ask, "Don't you know she's standing *right over there?*"

Texting appears to have replaced the art of live communication. That, I don't understand. Yes, it works beautifully for conversations like:

What time are we meeting?

9:30.

Okay.

But true communication requires *context*. Visual cues, body language, and facial expressions. Sometimes, what we have to say needs to be said In Real Life. Sometimes, we just need to put down the phone and *talk to each other*.

The Texting Never-Never List:

➢ **Angry texts**. "Pick up your damn phone!" "Where the HELL are you??" If you want to shout at me, do it when I can shout back or slam the door in your face. There's no sport in text-fighting.

➢ **Marriage proposals**. Seriously?? Unless you're in a war zone or under a mountaintop avalanche and these could possibly be your last words, "Will you marry me?" in a text is the least romantic proposal *ever*.

➢ **Breakup or Divorce texts**. "I love you, but it's just not working for me anymore." Or, "I'm leaving you for Porsche, our daughter's college roommate." What are you, like, twelve?? If you've spent twenty years together, bought a house and a dog, and had two kids with this woman, grow up and go *tell her* in person.

- **Group texts**. I hate these. Someone blasts a text out to you and a dozen or so people you don't know, who then proceed to have an on-going, active discussion amongst themselves, resulting in your text message notification beeper going off all. day. long.

- **Cryptic texts**. "Clinic just called with my test results back. Need to talk to you." "The police were just here. Call me." These require multiple back-and-forths, trying to get to the point. Save us all time and *call me* to tell me exactly what's going on.

- **Douche texts**. "Great to meet you last night. What's your friend's number?" Or, "Wife is out of town. Wanna hook up?" How about you give me your wife's number, buddy?

- **Idiot texts**. These include all texts to your drug dealer or your bookie. "Hey, I'm in the parking lot. Has the stuff arrived yet?" Or, "I lost again? Crap. I'll have your money tomorrow." It's been done.

- **Sexy texts** (or God forbid, **photo texts of your naked junk**) to someone other than your wife. Ask any politician how this one ends.

- **Bad news texts**. "You're fired." Or, "Wrecked your car, dude." Just bad form.

- **Premature texts**. "I love you," when neither of you has said it before. It lacks a little… Well, it lacks everything.

- **Trash-talking texts**. "Suzie is such a slut." Or, "What does she see in that guy? He's a pig." You now have no plausible deniability that you said those things. And once it's in someone's message box, you have no control over who *that* person sends them to. This would include sending it to Suzie. Or the pig.

- ➢ **Death in the family**. This includes Binkie, the family cat. "At your house. I think your cat is dead," or, worse, "Great-aunt Bertha died. Call home" should *never* be delivered via typed message. Grab a bottle of wine, some tissues, and deliver this in person.

- ➢ **Apology texts**. A casual text for a minor indiscretion— "Sorry I didn't join up with you guys last night. Bad shrimp. Will call later"—is acceptable. But if you've really stepped in it and you need to undo something BIG, any attempts to make light or be cute will backfire. "Sry. I was a jerk 4 sleeping with yr sister. 4give?" is just tacky.

- ➢ **The deep texts**. Trying to resolve or debate anything more significant than what time to meet at the restaurant after work via texting is stupid. Long, complicated texts are hard to read and require the reader to reply with something equally pithy. If you want to talk about the meaning of life or whether or not you should splurge on that rockin' black leather jacket, come over. I'll pour the wine.

- ➢ **Sarcastic texts**. If you're pissed off because he forgot to pick up the wine on the way home or he forgot to tell you he was bringing four guests over for dinner, texting a "Thanks for thinking about *me*, jackass" will only feel satisfying until you come face-to-face with this person again. Sarcasm can take a minor annoyance and turn it into a full-fledged street brawl in sixty seconds flat.

- ➢ **Drunk texts**. Anything you have to say after more than three drinks or after midnight, whichever comes first. This includes jokes (trust me, they won't still be funny in the morning), rants to your boss (the only time when "You're fired" texts can be appropriate), or drunk begging to an ex you want back (yeah, *that* won't be humiliating at breakfast).

So please, every once in a while, put down your phone. Or better yet, turn it off. Then, let's go have lunch and talk to each other, just like in the old days.

"Be nice to your daughter-in-law.

She's sleeping with the man who will pick out your nursing home."

~ Anonymous

13 Mistakes You Might be Making with Your Daughter-in-Law

LAST NIGHT, I watched *Monster-in-Law*, where Jane Fonda plays the mother of a young man who falls in love and marries a lovely young woman. Mama Jane is determined not to be replaced as the most important woman in her son's life and proceeds to hilariously undermine their relationship at every possible turn. It all works out in the end, but I couldn't help laughing over the lengths Mom went to ensure she wasn't going to become invisible or unnecessary.

The immense popularity of this comedy tells me that many mothers of sons identified with Ms. Fonda's predicament. The saying "A daughter is a daughter all of her life, but a son is a son until he takes a wife" can set Moms up to make extreme emotional adjustments in the blink of an eye. We've watched, prodded, helicopter parented, loved, and fiercely protected our boy for two or more decades, and now we're just "Mom" on his iPhone speed dial list.

From Jane Fonda in *Monster-in-Law* to Marie in *Everybody Loves Raymond*, MILs have taken a big hit. There are entire comedy shticks on TV and in nightclubs about the horrible mother-in-law who tries to ruin her son's marriage. But it's not that we're trying to *ruin* it. We just want to feel *part* of it.

Thankfully, there comes a time when we ultimately realize that the best way to stay in our beloved son's life is to keep the DIL happy. You love *him*, but he loves *her*. Happiness and a Welcome mat by their front door are best achieved by trying to avoid these conversational landmines during your next mother-daughter outing:

1. **"When are you two going to give me a grandbaby?"** Even if you could un-see the disturbing visual this conversation immediately evokes of your son and his wife doing the skippy every night, "trying to make a baby," this is, quite frankly, none of your business. And constant reminders from you that "you're not getting any younger" will never put more yippy in their skippy.

2. **"You're going to name the baby *what*?"** Yeah, just what they need. A butt-hurt phone call from you demanding to know why you're naming Baby Girl after *her* grandmother, the one who "never even comes to visit."

3. **"Why is the TV in front of that window? You should move it over there. And black towels in the bathroom??"** Back off, Mom. This isn't your house, and, if you ever want to be invited back, the only response to her floor plans, decorating styles, or color schemes should be "I love it."

4. **"Why do you have to live next door to *your* parents? We never get to see you, but *they* see you every day."** Stop whining. There could be a dozen practical reasons why they live where they do, and it doesn't have anything to do with whose parents they like more. Don't make this a competition with her parents. You'll lose.

5. **"I saw a wonderful book on cooking basics that I think you could use. I ordered it for you."** As a general rule, self-improvement books aimed at your DIL are a bad idea. *Bad.* Whether you think she's not a good cook, she needs to lose weight, or she doesn't have a grasp on parenting, this will not end well. Even the most devoted mama's boy will dump his mother like a hot biscuit if she starts criticizing his wife.

6. **"It's just my opinion, but I think you should…"** Whatever is coming next, Stop. Talking. Everyone knows that that sentence is a preamble to something she's doing *wrong.* A compliment never begins with "It's just my opinion." And "I think you should…" is passive-controlling. Double fail.

7. **"Why does little Sally *do* that??"** Watching your granddaughter repeatedly bang her spoon on the table while she eats and then looking confused or irritated while you question DIL about why she "lets" her daughter misbehave is likely to get you ejected from the kitchen. Sometimes, kids like to make noise. Yours did, too.

8. **"How can you let Billy eat that stuff? When *my* son was little, I never gave him sugar."** Well, good for you. But Billy isn't your son. He's hers. Unless she's feeding him a steady stream of Ding Dongs and Red Bull, Billy will grow up just fine.

9. **"I know you told me not to let Suzie stay up until eleven, but I figured it would be okay because she was with Grandma."** If DIL told you not to do something, *don't.* Respect the boundaries that your son and DIL have set, or your visits with the little darlings may start being supervised by one of the parents.

10. **"You two shouldn't be spending your money on tattoos. You have other bills to pay."** How do you know what they have to spend? Unless you're their bookkeeper or they *asked* for your advice, their spending habits are none of your business. Even today, could your checkbook register withstand critiquing from *your* parents?

11. **"In my day, we controlled our kids. Our parents spanked us, so we learned right from wrong."** Advising a young mother to whack her kids every time they act out is archaic and unhelpful. If you really want to score points (and you're such an expert), take the kids for the afternoon and send DIL to the day spa for some quiet time.

12. **"Your house could use a good cleaning. I've got some great products I'll bring over."** So she's either lazy and doesn't care or she's inept and doesn't know how to clean. That little jab will be rehashed with her husband at dinner for three hours, until he calls, asking why you made his wife cry.

13. **"My son would never have said that if you hadn't provoked him."** Get real, Mom. Some days, even your wonderful, talented, smart boy can be a total jackass. It happens. And blaming every tiff on her can quickly become the two of them angry with *you*. You're right. It's not fair. But who ever said love is?

"Style is a way to say who you
are
without having to speak."

~ Rachel Zoe

10 Things You Need to Get Out of Your Closet

Right Now

CALL A RANDOM list of a dozen women you know and ask them if they've ever thrown out anything from their Hubs's closet that he persisted in wearing five years after it died. Ratty T-shirts, saggy sweatpants, pilled sweaters, stained sweatshirts. Nine women will admit that yes, they've secretly tossed an item or two into the alley dumpster while hubby was at work. And of the three who deny it, one of them is lying. It appears we are much better at keeping *his* closet free of clutter than we are our own.

For many years, I was a freelance public speaker for women's groups in British Columbia and the Pacific Northwest. Over the years, I've given dozens of humorous after-lunch or dinner talks on confidence crises, weight struggles, beauty angst, marriage etiquette, and how to avoid embarrassing wardrobe malfunctions. I *loved* it (and still do). I spoke to cooking groups, book clubs, equestrian clubs, professional organizations, craft circles, and an entire female branch of traditional men's groups, all ending in "-ettes." (Remember, this was circa 1980: Kiwanettes and Lionettes did, in fact, exist.)

The most frequently requested topic was "Declutter Your Closet & Simplify Your Life." Apparently, closet streamlining was an issue for women *everywhere*, with no respect for age, income, or job status. Our bond of sisterhood was firmly grounded in a universal inability to get in there and start tossing crap out. "I don't know where to start!" was the lament I heard from women in two countries and three states.

So, for those of you who ever feel frustrated, depressed, or lost, standing in front of an overstuffed, "can't cram one more thing in there, but still don't have anything to *wear*" closet, here are some guidelines to get you started. Grab a bottle of wine (trust me, it will help smooth things along), and say "Buh-bye, baby" to the following:

1. **Anything that used to fit or might fit at some undetermined time in the future but doesn't fit *now*.** Especially if it requires losing the same number of pounds you've been working on since 1984. This includes pieces that you tell yourself will look great again after you "lose the pregnancy weight." And your kid is twenty-seven.

2. **Anything for a life you no longer have.** Yes, fifteen years ago, you and hubby were the hottest couple on the dance floor. You love that dress almost as much as you love Hubs. But three kids and a couple of decades later, "going out" means a 4:00 matinee, Papa Murphy's pizza, and bed by 8:30. Even if you *could* still get into it, it won't look the same. Gravity, age, menopause, and questionable lifestyle choices change our bodies, if not in size, in *shape*. If that LBD "fits," but requires full-body Spanx that compress you like a cocktail weenie to zip it up, and a full-coverage, Kevlar underwire granny bra to get your breasts back up off your waist, it's time for it to go.

3. **Period pieces or fads**. Prairie skirts, acid-wash jeans, or shimmery spandex leotards with leg warmers. Anything that sets your adult offspring into fits of uncontrolled hilarity when they see your college photo albums. And people who tell you "everything comes back into style eventually" were not talking about acid-wash jeans.

4. **Event-specific items**. Cheerleading skirts, bridesmaid's dresses, costume parties, old wedding dresses (particularly to a man to whom you are not currently married; that's just tacky). If the sentimental value is so overwhelming that you need to keep it forever, box it up and put it in the attic with all the other junk your kids are going to throw out shortly after your unfortunate demise.

5. **Anything your twenty-two-year-old DIL wants to borrow**. If she's all "It's, like, OMG, like, *fabulous*," it fits her, and it *suits her age*, YOU shouldn't be wearing it. Period.

6. **Styles you love but in colors that don't work for you**. Hint: If every time you wear that mauve sweater, four people tell you you look tired or ask if you're feeling well, the color is wrong. You can't fix it. Women tell me, "I'll get a different lipstick." Or, "I'll wear it with a scarf." Now you've made it worse. If the color washes you out, changing your makeup or adding another piece of clothing that blends with the sweater is just adding insult to injury.

7. **Anything you have to fuss with**. If you're constantly adjusting the waistband, pulling up the shoulder strap, or unwedgie-ing the fabric up your butt, *it doesn't fit*. And it can be awkward trying to explain your hand down your pants when running into your ex at the liquor store.

8. **More than one outfit for cleaning the basement or planting the garden.** Oversized, faded, ratty clothes are comfy, but an entire wardrobe of these T-shirts makes it too tempting to live in them on days you're *not* planting the back forty.

9. **Anything torn or dirty that needs repairs, alterations, or cleaning, but will never get any of those things.** If it's been in disrepair for eight years, you're not going to fix it. Give it to someone who will or who doesn't care if the hem is held up with staples.

10. **Anything someone else bought for you (Hubby, MIL, sister) that you hate and will never wear, *ever*.** If you just can't toss it because you'll be struck by lightning and go to bad-wife hell, box it up and put it in the attic with the dress from your wedding to Thor during your WWE-Raw-groupie phase in college. If anyone asks, just say, "It's at the dry cleaners." That'll give you time to drag it out in a panic.

And now, as you're standing in front of your empty closet, buck naked, wailing, *"But now I have nothing to wear,"* you may be right. So slip on your favorite T-shirt and yoga pants (c'mon, we all keep those) and gas up the car. Shopping road trip? Oh, yeah.

"Old age is like flying through a storm.
Once you're aboard,
there's nothing you can do."

~ Golda Meir

From Cougar to Crazy Cat Lady.
Has it Happened to You?

SEVERAL YEARS ago, around the mid-'70s, Gail Sheehy wrote a book called *Passages*, where she described the various stages we go through during the decades from our twenties through our fifties. It was wildly popular and is still a top seller to people looking to understand the emotional process of aging.

Ms. Sheehy kind of wraps it up around fifty, but I think that some of the most dramatic changes happen *after* that. We start getting senior discounts. AARP starts stalking us with monthly applications for membership. And menopause keeps us busy with hot flashes, mood swings, fatigue, and chronic bitchiness to anybody within a twenty-five-foot radius.

One of the most difficult transitions often occurs during late menopause, when we realize that we are no longer "sexy" to anyone under seventy. Sure, they may call us "pretty" or even "beautiful." But flattering physical descriptions now end with the dreaded qualifier, "*for her age.*" "She looks great, for sixty-five" or, "She's still gorgeous, for her age."

It's no secret that we live in a society that worships youth. Our social barometer for "hot" includes tanned skin, perky boobs, tight abs, cellulite-free butts, and legs like a *Sports Illustrated* swimsuit model. The only good news is, as baby boomers got older, we collectively raised the bar to include "cougars," "MILFs," and even "GILFs," meaning sexually attractive women up to the age of forty-five or fifty.

But there comes a time when our adult son's friends start seeing us less as Mrs. Robinson from *The Graduate*, and more Mrs. Cunningham from *Happy Days*. Our Match.com profile would primarily attract men who could lecture about prostate malfunctions and the merits of Cialis versus Viagra better than the local pharmacist. Yes, we've reached the age where we must gracefully concede that our youthful hotness has left the building and is never coming back. (Demi Moore, are you listening?)

But how do you know if it's time? Watch for these signs:

- **You buy your underwear for comfort rather than foreplay**. It's full butt, no frills, with spandex panels for firming your Buddha Belly and your jiggly butt. Hubby has seen you in them, and you don't care.

- **You're buying a new convertible, in black**, because the red one makes you feel like a sixty-something woman trolling for a job at Hooters.

- **You're the oldest person in your office**. And your age and medical condition raise your co-worker's group healthcare premiums.

- **You've stopped flirting with the UPS guy** because even thinking about an affair is exhausting. You'd rather take a nap.

- **You have fifteen pairs of reading glasses**, because you like your accessories to match your outfit.

- **Your grandkids set you up on Twitter, but you never use it** because to "tweet" someone sounds slightly pornographic.

- You *have* grandkids.

- **You saw a nose/ear hair trimmer at Walgreens and considered buying one.** (Or two, so you'll have one in your travel bag.)

- **Pajama Pants begin to look like an actual clothing option**. In public.

- **Your Saturday night plans take into account Sunday morning**. Recovery time becomes the determining factor in the festivities agenda.

- **$85 for a moisturizer** that promises to smooth fine lines and "take years of your face" seems reasonable.

- **A night of board games, in your fleece jammies with Hubs,** is more appealing than a night out on the town.

- **You got a Snuggie for Christmas**, and you love it.

- **You've developed a sudden obsession with gardening.** This is often accompanied, during the winter, by an uncontrollable need to collect Chia Pets.

- **The hair on your head and legs is thinning,** but now you're finding stubby black strays coming from your chin, your nose, and "*OMG*, is that one sprouting out of my nipple??" (see #8)

- **You have morning aches and pains**, but you didn't do anything physical the day before. And you've stopped telling people it's "a pulled muscle."

- **Doctors, lawyers, and policemen all start to look seventeen**. Seriously, were they *all* child prodigees?

- **Daily naps take the place of daily workouts**. Naps make you happy.

- Shopping sprees that used to focus on LBDs and stilettos are now hunts for yoga pants and running shoes. Even though you already have eight pairs of yoga pants. In black.

- Your Kegal exercises are more about bladder control than sex. Hubby is thrilled, and we're not telling.

- You can no longer pass the "Pencil Test." (i.e., Place a pencil horizontally under your butt cheek and see whether it falls to the ground or if your droopy cheeks hold it up.) The last time you tried it, you could hold three magic markers under one cheek alone. Winning.

- You must consciously resist the overwhelming urge to slap the next twenty-two-year-old Barbie who insists that she wants to "grow old naturally." Just you wait, Babs. Someday *this* body will be yours.

- Your legs have more red and blue lines than the American flag, and you're afraid to wear white because everyone will assume you're a runaway float ornament from the 4th of July parade.

- You started keeping copious To-Do lists around the house, once it became apparent that the only thing you can remember to do is eat.

- You go to bed at 8:30 every night. Friends and family know, if there's no fire or blood, don't call after 8 p.m.

- You discover that sex, in the afternoon and without alcohol, is pretty damn good.

When I turned fifty, my father mentioned, "You know you're officially old when you turn fifty."

"No," I replied, "you know you're officially old when your *kids* turn fifty." Boom.

"If women are so bloody perfect
at multitasking,
how come they can't
have a headache and sex
at the same time?"

~Billy Connolly

How to Seduce Your Wife

A FEW WEEKS ago, I posted a piece called "Not Tonight Dear, I Have a Headache," listing some of the things men do that can torpedo a woman's desire to get nekkid and hit the sheets with their partners. A short time later, I received a message from a gentleman that said, "Great list, but I must be a total tool, because I do most of those things. Now I know what not to do. But what *do* I do?"

Oh, this is going to be fun.

Dear Tool Guy,

Glad you asked! But before we get into practical tips, you need to understand that men and women are *different*. Especially when it comes to sex. You guys are mostly visual, and all you need is a naked, willing body and a smile, and it's yippee time (fyi, we occasionally get jealous about that). We like a little foreplay, emotional as well as physical. We want to feel loved, appreciated, noticed, and desirable, even when we're not naked. If you can do that, we'll rock your world on a regular basis.

With that in mind, try these:

❖ **Be more affectionate *before* sex is anticipated**. Ignoring us all day long until bedtime then giving us "the wink" tends to make us feel like a life-size blowup doll. A friend of mine says her husband claims it "help him sleep better." "Swell," she says with a sigh. "I'm a human Ambien."

❖ **Do something to brighten her day other than offering her your awesome body.** Wash her car. Do the laundry. Take the kids to the park while she gets a massage or lunches with a girlfriend. Trust me: next time you have an afternoon quickie, it'll be *her* idea.

❖ **Ask her about her day. Then *listen*.** Respond with full sentences rather than monosyllabic grunts and head nods. Extra points if you turn off the TV while you're talking.

❖ **Make her laugh.** It's the greatest aphrodisiac *ever*.

❖ **Go the extra mile.** Remember dating, when you looked good, smelled great, and had breath that smelled like spearmint instead of stale beer? Yeah, that.

❖ **Touch, but don't grope.** Grabbing our boobs as we're walking past you with a load of dirty laundry is one of the fastest ways to ensure you're sleeping with the dog between you in the master bed that night. Groping is not foreplay. It's annoying. Touching, however, with a long hug or a slow kiss, can melt her heart and weaken her knees. And if you really want to seal the deal, take that load of laundry from her hands and get it done while she has a bubble bath. Gratitude sex can be even better than makeup sex.

❖ **Don't confuse us with porn stars.** Women prefer "sexy sex." We want a little seduction, not a B-rated porno production from late-night pay-per-view. Remember, porn is written largely for men, by men, so all you're seeing is what turns *you guys* on, not us. If you're not sure what gets our motors revving, *ask*. We might even show you something new.

❖ **Pay attention**. It's in the details, Tool Guy. Is she almost out of her favorite wine? Is there a Post-It note on the fridge, reminding her to pick up the dry cleaning? Are you running low on the coffee she always buys for you? If you're out and about, pick up the wine. Get the dry cleaning. Buy your own coffee. She'll notice that *you* noticed. We like that. A lot.

❖ **Surprise her by doing something from her "marital chore list."** No one wants to cook seven damn dinners every week, all year long, or do all the laundry, every day, for everyone living under the roof. Every now and then, let her sip wine while you cook. (And ordering pizza is *not* the same thing.) And if you clean up afterwards, paradise will await you, just down the hall.

❖ **Treat her the way you did when you were dating**. Carry the groceries in. Put the toilet seat down. Hold the door open for her instead of charging in ahead of her and letting it smack her in the face. (Stand in the doorway at Safeway. You'll see this one more often than you think.) Be the gentleman your mama taught you to be.

❖ **Give her genuine compliments without immediately tying it to sex**. "You look beautiful tonight," and then *stop talking*—that's perfect. "You look hot tonight. Wanna do it?" pretty much obliterates anything you might have achieved. It reduces the conversation to, "I'll tell you something nice so you'll have sex with me." After age twenty, you need a smoother approach.

❖ **Touch her even when you're not suggesting sex**. That's the #1 complaint I hear from women. "He only touches me when he wants sex." After a certain point, she starts to feel like one of Pavlov's dogs, where, every time you touch her, she's supposed to keel over onto her back. She'll quickly find a way to avoid your touches altogether.

❖ **When she is ready, try to slow down, Cowboy.** Don't rush to the "good part." We think the journey is as good as the destination. Give her time to catch up with you, and I promise she'll put the yippy back in your skippy.

You're welcome, Tool Guy. And remember: Happy wife, happy life!

*"Raising kids is part joy
and part guerilla warfare."*

~Ed Asner

Bake Sale Moms
Ruling the Schools Since 1989

LAST WEEKEND, our son and his wife came to visit, bringing their two small children. We sat around the dining table, happily chatting about everything and nothing. Eventually, the subject got around to the wee ones' schooling and the expected level of commitment from parents and grandparents in fund-raising events. Including the dreaded Bake Sale.

I had a flashback to the moment when my son, barely finished with his first-grade orientation, rushed through the door and thrust a semi-clean piece of crumpled paper into my hands, announcing an upcoming bake sale. All mothers were expected to contribute. And it needed to be from scratch. *And* creatively presented. Oh, and it was tomorrow.

I don't cook. I hate it. I knew by eighth grade that it was not for me, when all my giggling girlfriends were eager for Home Ec class while I opted for wood shop with Billy Butz (who spent most of the year in detention due to his unfortunate habit of fondling his junk at recess), which shows you how far I was willing to go. Twenty years later, I found myself holding what would be the first of a ridiculous number of flyers over the years, handed out with knowing and superior smiles by the *Bake Sale Moms*.

These women are tough. And they take their bake sales *very* seriously. They think nothing of giving you less than twenty-four hours between the wadded notice and the presentation of your famous Disney princess cookie collection, because *their* bake-off artwork has been ready since last Tuesday. These women compete fiercely every year for imaginary first place, jockeying for position to determine who can bring in the most beautiful, well-presented, or most complicated recipe. Winners and runners-up are chosen by the self-appointed pack leader, with categories in "first to sell," "most money paid," or "best presentation." This hierarchy remains absolute and unwavering until the next bake-off.

There's no room in this club for women who don't bake. You'll never know their secret handshake or be invited to any of their get-togethers, because, well, *you* don't know the difference between real vanilla and imitation. *You* don't understand why someone would spend $11 on an entire jar of cardamom when the recipe only calls for 1/8 of a tablespoon. *You don't belong.* So you humbly offer up a paper plate of slightly burnt, generic chocolate chip cookies, obviously sliced from a frozen log, which totally humiliates your child, brings in a paltry two bucks from the janitor in a pity sale, and gets yourself permanently banned from the prestigious Bake Sale Moms' Club.

When my son was in second grade, we were living in Maui, in an uber-cute, plantation-style house surrounded by old banana trees. Less *Gone with the Wind* and more 140-year-old sharecropper's cottage, it came with original plumbing *and* appliances. Quaint, but not without some inconveniences.

One day, he came home from school and announced that I was supposed to bake some cookies for the bake sale that was, oh yeah, tomorrow. Trying not to panic, since I didn't have a clue how to get started (and those "I make *my* child his own Christmas tree every year using toilet paper tubes and glitter" moms can be flat-out scary), I decided to at least attempt to fit in and make my kid proud.

I discovered we actually had a cookbook with cookie recipes (who knew?), so I sat down to find one that didn't ask for some weird "cream of tartar" or include a thirteen-page tutorial at the bottom on how to use pointy tubes of frosting to draw animal faces on your cookies because, "Wouldn't that just be, like, adorable??" (For the love of God, who *are* these women??)

I finally found one that looked simple enough, and I set all the ingredients out on kitchen table, ready to dazzle my young progeny.

Step one: Preheat oven to 350. Hmmm. There were five knobs on the front. When I turned the one that said "Temp," all I heard was a hissing sound from inside the oven. I may not be Martha in the kitchen, but I was pretty sure ovens were not supposed to *hiss*. I called a girlfriend, who asked if the pilot light was on.

"What the hell is a 'pilot light?'" I asked.

"You have a gas oven," she explained, "You need to light the pilot light inside the oven to turn it on." All righty, then. Historically, kitchens and anything flaming have not worked out well for me, but this was for my boy, so I was going in.

I quickly realized I had absolutely no idea where this mysterious pilot light might be, so I flicked on a long, candle-type lighter, opened the oven door, stuck the lighter in and waved it around, hoping it would somehow figure out where to go so I could get chopping on my bragging rights.

The next thing I heard was an extremely loud **BANG**, immediately followed by a **WHOOSH** of thick, greasy, black smoke billowing out of the oven and streaming oily black soot on me, the walls, the table, all my ingredients, and Poi, the mangy (and now seriously pissed) plantation cat that had happened to stroll by looking for treats. Well, crap.

Jake was standing in the doorway, doubled over with laughter, with all the glee of a six-year-old whose mother has just completely torched her kitchen for his personal amusement. He chortled, "Boy, the other mothers aren't going to *believe* this. We should take a picture of you, Mom. This is *great!!*"

Awesome. I told him to give me an hour to clean up the mess, take a shower, and hose down the cat. Then we were off to Safeway for some Oreos. Bite me, bake sale.

And now the next generation is bringing home those same damn flyers. Screw it. If those Betty Crocker wannabes don't want my Oreos, I'm bringing wine. Bet those mothers can't make *that*.

"When you see a married couple
walking down the street,
the one that's a few steps ahead
is the one that's mad."

~Helen Rowland

Marriage, Phase 1: How to Tell if It's Gone

(And Why You Might Want it Back)

I LOVE love. We all love love. Especially new love. Your heart beats faster when your partner pulls into the driveway. You get all giddy when your phone rings and you see that it's him. You love the tiny laugh lines around his eyes and the way his skin smells. Even his breathing fascinates you.

That's called "Phase 1." It's a near-constant state of romantic euphoria, during which you risk an Amish shunning by your girlfriends if you don't stop waxing poetic about how amazing, gorgeous, and great in bed your new man is and don't they all wish they were you. Phase 1 is filled with delightful discoveries about each other every day. There's a level of uncertainty and newness about the relationship and your future together.

This doesn't last.

After a few years, the newness inevitably begins to fade. We know (really, we *know*) our partners. We've seen them in every possible state and condition. We've heard their stories, and we know the punchline to all their favorite jokes. We know where all their family skeletons are buried. We know what they like and don't like to eat and how they take their morning coffee. Nothing is off-limits or private. We're now in "Phase 2."

Phase 2 can be every bit as loving and joyful as Phase 1. And it does give us a kind of "marital street cred" by having achieved this emotional comfort level together. But many couples cite the loss of intensity or intrigue as a contributing factor to the decreased passion in the marriage. Combined with the feeling that we know *everything* there is to know about our spouse, it can begin to feel like we're married to our best buddy. Or our brother.

How do you know if it might be time to get a little Phase 1 back into the marriage?

- ❖ **When you talk about him to your girlfriends, you frequently mention that "relationships aren't always unicorns and glitter."** Any woman over forty knows what you really mean is, "Harold is a jerk when he's stressed, and he's *always* stressed. I want you all on my jury after I snuff him in his sleep."

- ❖ **You openly criticize him in public.** Instead of the daily soliloquies on his amazingness, you now start girls' lunch conversations with, "He thinks I want to go *fishing* with him. Is he an idiot or what??"

- ❖ **Little quirks or jokes that used to seem endearing or funny, which he repeats to everyone you meet, now make you want to smack him.** You find yourself thinking, "If he does that snort-laugh *one. more. time,* I'm going to scream." Or, "If he tells that shopping joke to another sales clerk, he's going *down.*"

- ❖ **The sex has become predictable or repetitive. Or nonexistent.** If you have sex with the TV turned up so you can hear the next episode of *The Walking Dead* from the bedroom, it might be time to have a chat with Hubby.

While it's true we're not the randy rabbits we were in our youth, if you need to check your day-planner for the last time you had sex, you might want to make sure that that's the last time *he* had it, too.

❖ **You haven't shut the bathroom door since 2009.** There are some activities that we simply should do in private. That's why builders put doors between the bedroom and the bathroom. Rooms with toilets visible from the beds are called jail cells. Doing your potty business, popping menopausal pimples, or squishing your thighs to check for cellulite are all better done without an audience. When he fantasizes about getting you under the sheets, he doesn't need the visual stuck in his head of you yanking out chin hairs with tweezers.

❖ **You no longer say "I love you."** This isn't about the shout-out from down the hall when he's leaving for work or the automatic "Love you/Love you, too" couple's phone sign-off. I'm talking about the last time you stopped what you were doing, put down your phone, looked him in the eyes, and said, "I. Love. You." Big difference. *Big.*

❖ **You actively watch TV or text while talking to each other.** This is rude and dismissive. I don't even try to talk to Hubs while he's watching Gonzaga play, because it *pisses me off* when I'm trying to talk to him and he keeps glancing at the TV like he can't wait for me to shut up. (He says he feels the same way when we're in the middle of a conversation and I start texting the kids. I get it.)

❖ **You no longer have random displays of affection.** You used to hold hands in public. You touched each other. A hand on the arm. A quick hug or light kiss. (Not to be confused with drunken make-outs that result in people shouting instructions to "Get a room.") Spontaneous, outward signs of intimacy have gone away, and you can't remember when that happened. But now, holding hands seems juvenile and PDAs are *embarrassing*. You feel like you're being groped in the produce department. Apparently, he agrees.

❖ **When you fight, it's no longer cute.** Fights during Phase 1 usually end quickly, with a coy "Oh my God, are we *fighting*?" immediately followed by enthusiastic make-up sex. Real-life fights in a marriage can be smackdowns that include off-limits references to Hubby's dead grandmother's obnoxious alcoholic uncle and how Hubby is behaving *just like him*. Chalk up another sexless night in your day-planner.

❖ **You don't laugh together anymore.** Your conversations have become limited to your overdrawn checking account, the kids' education expenses, your jerk of a boss and how you could do his job in your sleep, or Hairball, the family cat and whether his chronic irritable bowel syndrome means you need to put him down. Your relationship, while "stable," isn't *fun* anymore.

Now, before you start shouting at me that you and your hubby share every intimate detail and bodily function and you're still crazy in love, I think that's wonderful. By all means, carry on. I'll go sit quietly in the corner with a doughnut and a Diet Coke. But if you've ever felt like you're married to your brother, consider closing the bathroom door. You might like what happens next.

"A gourmet meal without a glass
of wine
just seems tragic to me
somehow."

~Kathy Mattea

20 Reasons Everything is Better with Wine

THOSE OF YOU who know me personally or who read my column (thank you!) know that I love red wine. I love the beautiful, swirling colors, the oaky fragrance, the warmth of that first sip of a good vintage, the subtle differences between varietals, and even the sexy, long-stemmed glasses. (Actually, the long-stemmed glasses are a fantasy. Kind of like a Norman Rockwell painting of the perfect, harmonious family dinner: a lovely visual, but a tad short on reality. I'm such a klutz that the household stemware collection has been exchanged, over the years, for fat-bottom tumblers and old jam jars. But the sentiment remains intact.)

In my experimental years, I tried white wines (sharp and cold), tropical mixed drinks (fruit punch with a nasty kick), sophisticated martini-type drinks (extremely bitter; who drinks these?), and hot drinks (the coffee kept me up for three days). If I don't like it, I'm not drinking it. The point has never been to get all sloshed on whatever's available and do stupid things I'd regret the next day, if I could remember them.

If red wine is not available, I'm the designated driver. But if there's a great cabernet on the menu, call a cab, because this woman is carrying a corkscrew. I do love a glass (or two... occasionally, three; don't judge) of red wine at the end of the day, winding down and chatting with Hubs about whatever comes to mind. Over the past few decades together, I've discovered many reasons to fall in love with my red wine.

1. *It's always there for you.* A bad day and nobody's home? Have a glass of wine. It'll all be better tomorrow.

2. *It's good for your heart.* I love the doctor who came up with this one.

3. *It's cheaper than a therapist.* My therapist charges $150/hour. I can get a fabulous bottle of Old Vine Zin for $12.

4. *You can drink it at home in your pajama pants and bunny slippers.* This works better if you're home alone. And you're not having breakfast.

5. Depending on your mood, *you can drink it out of a beautiful glass, straight from the bottle, or out of a box.* Yeah, that's come in handy more than once.

6. *You can find it wherever you get your prescriptions refilled* for feminine itching products. (And on the third bout of that unfortunate itch, trust me: you'll be needing that second bottle.)

7. *It makes you sound sophisticated* when you drop words like "legs," "bouquet," and "tone." Don't worry if you don't know what those actually mean. Just stick them in a sentence when you hold up your glass or take a sip. Nobody else knows, either.

8. *It makes you look classy.* Well, at least during the first two glasses. After that, you're on your own.

9. *It can help you bust your best dance moves.* But if those are the only inhibitions you plan to shed that night, after Ms. Summer finishes the "Last Dance," you should have a cab waiting.

10. *It helps you tolerate crazy relatives.* Grab a glass with a generous pour and find your Zen place. Preferably before Aunt Gertrude arrives and asks, for the two hundredth time, why her gardening club in Minnesota hasn't heard of your book.

11. *You can make fun words for new activities.* Camping + wine = Glamping. Hiking + wine = Wiking. These are actual descriptions of activities offered in the Pacific Northwest. Personally, I'd much rather glamp than camp, and wike than hike. (Then, of course, there's banking + wine = Wanking. *Bahahahaha.* I crack myself up.)

12. *If you're in the mood for more than one glass, wine tastings are available at any winery.* Tastings are a socially acceptable way to have twelve glasses in front of you with no fear of judgment, because so does everybody else.

13. *It helps you have conversations with people who make no sense.* "I have no clue what you just said. Let me go get another glass of wine, and you can explain it to me again" is perfectly acceptable. If the other person is really an idiot, you can get two.

14. *It helps you get through a six-hour family reunion* without hyperventilating into a paper bag in the bathroom. (Okay, maybe that's just me.)

15. *It's the perfect gift for almost any occasion.* Birthdays, anniversaries, housewarmings, and the day you spayed Boots, the family cat. Everybody loves a celebration.

16. *It can bring a group together like nobody's business*. Eight women at a table is fun. Eight women at a table with two bottles of a great malbec is a party.

17. *It's fun*. Science tells us that red wine releases endorphins, the "happy hormones" that make everything better. Kind of like running, but you don't have to get out of your sand chair on the beach.

And it just keeps getting better…

18. *Studies also show that two glasses per day can slow dementia, reduce depression, and increase our sex drive*. It's a wine trifecta. I'm so proud of you, my yummy little glass of cabernet.

19. A recent study found that **women who drink red wine were less likely to gain weight** over a thirteen-year period of time. Jenny Craig vs. Nutrisystem? Who cares?

20. *It gets better with age*. (And gives us hope that we will, too.)

"You see much more of your children after they leave home."

~Lucille Ball

Empty Nest. First, You Cry.
Then You Laugh

"EMPTY NEST." Every parent knows what that means. Some dread it. Some look forward to it. Either way, if you have kids, it's going to happen. It's normal and natural for our children to leave home somewhere between eighteen and twenty-two years of age and begin life as reasonably sane, independent adults. But, after almost two decades of guiding and watching over our young progeny, laughing, loving, disciplining, cheering victories, and healing heartaches, how do we let them walk out the door with a breezy, "Bye, Mom," all their worldly goods, and most of our checking account?

Most people agree it would be a bit weird to have a healthy, grown child who never left home. He'd eventually become that creepy guy in all those movies about the forty-two-year-old man living with his mother in the big house up on the hill. *Failure to Launch* was a hilarious movie about a young man refusing to leave the convenience and affordability of living with his parents. The success of this film was an indication of its resonance with both generations.

Since it seems to be inevitable under normal circumstances, however, how do we celebrate, rather than mourn, the empty nest? Like most difficult things in life, we need to look for the silver lining. Yes, I understand that young Bradford the third is taking a year to trek the Himalayas with three friends, one backpack, and a Sherpa, and that baby Bitsy is going to the University of Five-Hours-Away-by-Plane, but you know what? You'll be okay. So put down that spoon, stick the Häagen-Dazs Triple Brownie Delight back in the freezer, pour a glass of wine, and visualize the following:

> **Your house is no longer a free hotel** for mini-adults who apparently believe it also comes with complimentary housekeeping and laundry services.

> **You can read a book**. All of it. In one weekend.

> **You can travel to grown-up-people destinations**. No more Disneyland or kid-focused hotels.

> **You can eat out at restaurants** that don't have Happy Meals on the menu or changing stations in the bathrooms.

> **You can take up a new hobby**. Buy the loom you've always wanted and set it up in Prissy's pink bedroom. Paint the room bright purple. Install shelving for your creations. Don't feel guilty. This is *your* room now.

> **You can turn Samson's downstairs bedroom into a wine cellar**. Repeat after me. A. Wine. Cellar.

> **No more fighting over the remote** or yelling at selectively deaf teenagers to "Turn down the damn TV!"

> **Your mornings belong to *you***. No more lunches to pack, uniforms to wash, breakfasts to whip up, carpools to join, or homework to review. Just you, a hot cappuccino, and Buford, your rescue pug, enjoying a quiet sunrise. *Aaahhh.*

> **You can fill your fridge with the good stuff** that you couldn't afford to feed the kids. For the last four years, your kitchen has been the motherlode of gigantic bags of

chips, cheese puffs, and Hot Pockets, attracting teenage locusts from all over town because you have all the good shit. Now you can stock up on fresh seafood, Pepperidge Farm chocolate mint cookies, and cheeses that don't come in individual plastic wrappers. Go crazy. Toss it all into the cart.

> **You don't have to set a good example every day**. Let's be honest. Being a daily role model to teenagers who know everything is *tough*. By move-out day, we've taught them pretty much everything we can. Now they're out the door, we can be our real selves, doing stupid things without worrying about embarrassing our kids or having to explain why we should have known better.

> **You have more cash**. The constant, daily handing out of cash for unanticipated events will eventually trickle to the occasional frantic text request ("Mom, pls send $200 asap! Oh, luv u!"), and you can now afford a massage. And a facial. Every month.

> **Your kitchen is no longer an all-night diner**. Twenty-four-hour access is now limited to you and Hubs. And you can be reasonably certain that the other half of your Little Debbie's cupcake will still be there tomorrow morning, when you get up.

> **You no longer have to cook separate meals** because the baby hates anything green, the eldest is dieting and won't eat carbs, and your tweener has decided she won't eat anything that "can look at her."

> **You can actually sleep through the night**, rather than doze like a mama fruit bat, with ears open and eyes half closed, listening for the key in the lock that says seventeen-year-old Rutger is home safe (and so is your car).

➤ **You no longer have to spend hundreds of dollars on uniforms** for Filbert to wear out on the field, so you can watch your teenage baby get tackled, pummeled, and body-slammed every Friday night.

➤ **No more long-distance, all-day sports practices or cold, rainy, morning soccer matches**. Unplug the alarm clock, and snuggle under the warm, poofy comforter for another hour (or two).

➤ **You can ditch the minivan** and get a car you actually like. Feeling the need for a bright red, two-seater convertible? Or you think your neighbor's tiny electric car is the cutest thing *ever*? Yep, they're both wildly impractical. But what the hell? Drive whatever you want. You've earned it.

➤ **No more bulk buying**. Cancel that Costco membership. You no longer need twelve bottles of ketchup, a gallon of shampoo, and eighty-seven rolls of toilet paper in your house at all times.

➤ **You get to give advice to new moms**. You have parenting street cred. You've raised one or more "good ones," and new mothers, unlike your children, will actually *want* advice from you.

➤ **You're one step closer to grandchildren**. Those adorable miniature humans, with their silky-soft hair and clean-baby smell, whom you can love and spoil the crap out of and then hand back to their original owners to raise.

And so, Simba, the circle of life begins again.

"They call it 'Menopause' because 'Mad Cow Disease' was already taken."

~Author Unknown

Menopause Making You Crazy?

There's a Name for That

Experts often love to announce a "new discovery" that the general population has known for decades. Chocolate makes you feel good (ya think?). Red wine is good for you (*duh*). And menopause can make you crazy (this study took *how* many years??).

While doing some research for another essay, I did a quick scan through my MD stepdad's DSM-IV and found myself laughing out loud at the striking similarities between the names of certain disorders and menopause symptoms.

- **Adjustment Disorder**: Bursting into tears at every morning weigh-in because you've inexplicably gained ten pounds in five days and it's clinging to your belly with the tenacity of barnacles on a cruise liner.

- **Acute Stress Disorder**: You valiantly battle hot flashes, night sweats, fatigue, weight gain, and mood swings, but dissolve into a sobbing meltdown upon discovering your first chin hair.

- **Adverse Effect of Prescriptions**: Cankles from retaining water like a two-humped dromedary.

- **Age-Related Cognitive Decline**: That's... *Um*... Oh crap, what was the question?

- **Antisocial Personality Disorder**: When you're out with friends who are all having a raucous, great time, and all you want to do is crawl into bed and take a nap. Naps are good. Naps are better than people.

- **Anxiety Disorder**: Constant worry about whether or not you'll ever feel sexy or desirable again. Or whether you'll even care.

- **Alcohol-Related Disorder**: At my house, we call this therapy.

- **Binge-Eating Disorder**: Because you shouldn't drink on an empty stomach.

- **Bipolar Disorder**: When you're apologizing to Hubby for being such a bitch to live with during this time and how lucky you are to be married to him, at which point he confesses that he forgot to pick up wine on the way home and you go all postal on his loser ass.

- **Borderline Intellectual Functioning**: The way you see everybody else on most days.

- **Brief Psychotic Disorder**: When the twelve-year-old, porcelain-skinned sales clerk at Nordstrom sweetly suggests a $150 moisturizer for "mature skin," to target "all those lines around your eyes."

- **Catatonic Disorder**: The result of seeing your back fat for the first time.

- **Cannabis-Related Disorder**: Discovering that marijuana actually helps with your menopause symptoms but feeling awkward about firing up a doobie in front of your grandchildren.

- **Cognitive Disorder:** When you call a friend to complain that you can't find your phone. Yeah. The one you're using right now to tell her you can't find your phone.

- **Communication Disorder:** Difficulty remembering the right words to express how you're feeling, so resorting to indicative behaviors, like hanging out the car window with your Shiatsu to cool down, sobbing in your shower because you ran out of your favorite shampoo, or eating the entire bag of Oreos that you "bought for the grandkids."

- **Delusional Disorder:** Paying $35 for an anti-cellulite cream for your thighs, and actually believing it will work.

- **Dependent Personality Disorder:** Limiting your social circle to other menopausal women who understand that you weren't always a crazy, sweaty, moody bitch. You have a new tribe, because other people are just so *annoying*.

- **Disruptive Behavior Disorder:** Seismic mood swings that regularly send your family and your Chihuahua scrambling for cover to any room you're not in.

- **Exhibitionism:** The total willingness to pull your shirt up to cool your boobs whenever you pass a fan. Including the ones at the mall.

- **Expressive Language Disorder:** Bursting out, "Will somebody turn the heat down? Anybody? Aren't you all hot?? It's *TOO F***ING HOT IN HERE*," while out for a romantic dinner with your hubby.

- **Female Sexual Arousal Disorder:** Regularly fantasizing about Charlie Hunnam, even though you know you could be his mother. So what if your fantasies always include alcohol and dimmer switches?

- **Hygiene Disorder:** When you stop changing the sheets after every bout of night sweats, and just throw a towel over the whole mess and go back to bed.

- **Hypoactive Sexual Desire Disorder:** When Hubby starts to look like your brother. You haven't had sex in six months. And you're good with that.

- **Hallucinogen-Related Behavior:** The inability to see your midlife muffin top and exposed butt crack while wearing your favorite low-rise jeans.

- **Identity Problem:** When you find yourself begging the universe to give you a sign that this manic-depressive, irritable, sweaty woman with a Buddha belly, saggy boobs, and runaway nose hair who you see in the mirror every morning is not the "real you."

- **Impulse Control Disorder:** The inability to refrain from eating everything that can't outrun you, even with a body that now gains weight on one Cheeto and a Diet Coke.

- **Major Depressive Episode:** When you realize that you've exchanged periods for monthly bloating, during which even your full-butt granny panties have muffin top.

- **Motor Skills Disorder:** Uncontrollable head-smacking of everyone within ten feet of your bathroom scale.

- **Narcissistic Personality Disorder:** When it really *is* all about you. Your brain is continually consumed with, "Will this ever end? I don't deserve this. Why me, why now? Nobody understands me. Nobody is paying attention to *me*. God, it's hot in here. You're not hot?? Well, I'm dying here. Somebody *turn on the friggin' air conditioner*! I'M HOT!"

- **Nightmare Disorder**: Spending thirty minutes breaking a sweat wiggling into your Spanx, and then realizing you need to pee. *Right. Freaking. Now.*

- **Oppositional Defiant Disorder**: When your boobs persist in heading south like migrating geese, no matter how many isometric chest exercises you do to get them "back *up* there."

- **Partner Relational Problems**: He's breathing. "I can *hear* you." Seriously?? Does he have to be so *loud*? He's breathes all. the. time. STOP THAT. Maybe I'm being hormonal. Nope. He's obviously just trying to piss me off.

- **Phase of Life Problem**: You know you need a magnifying mirror to pluck the stray hairs from your upper lip, but the first time you saw your menopausal skin magnified by a power of five, you locked yourself in the bathroom for three days.

So go ahead, get a little crazy, if you feel like it. The good news? This, too, shall pass.

"I thought a relationship was
only for two people,
but obviously some people don't
know how to count."

~Author Unknown

The Idiot's Guide to Having an Affair

So you've met her. Maybe she works in your office. Maybe you bumped into her in the produce department at your local grocery store. Or maybe she runs the same route that you do every morning through the park. And you can't stop thinking about her.

It doesn't matter that you're married. What starts out as a "harmless" flirtation has now become perilously close to The Line, and you've spent hours rationalizing how you're going to cross it without feeling like a shmuck or, more importantly, without getting caught. You love your wife. You really do. And you don't want to hurt her or leave her. But this girl is just so hot, and *she wants you*. What's a guy to do?

Well, if you truly don't want to hurt your wife and end up going through one of those relationship-imploding "I don't know why. It just *happened*" discussions, rule #1 is Don't Get Caught. For those of you not experienced in this field, here are some helpful tips:

> ➤ **Find a woman with the same name as your spouse**. This helps ensure that you don't blurt out, "Yes, Tiffany, *yes*," the next time you're in bed with your wife, Carol.

➢ **Immediately start calling Brandee ("with two Es")
something you can also call your wife, to avoid
embarrassing gaffes.** Try "Oh-Baby," which makes sense,
since we're assuming most of your time with Ms. Brandee-
with-two-Es will be spent in the sack. (Seriously, do you
give a rat's behind about her schizo family, her creepy
hairless cat, or her job troubles down at the Big Willie's
Dine & Dash All-Night Truckstop?) And if you slip and
call Wifey "Oh-Baby," she'll just assume it's a weird new
affectation from your obvious midlife crisis.

➢ **Buy two of every piece of jewelry you buy for Oh Baby.**
Expensive, yes. But that way, when your wife finds a
jewelry receipt, it will be for something you actually gave
her.

➢ **Never tell your wife you're "working late."** Many
marriages have imploded because a loving wife went to
Hubby's office to surprise him with dinner, only to
discover he'd left hours ago. With Oh-Baby. Much better
to say, "I got a flat tire and, while I was changing it, I was
attacked by a pack of pissed-off raccoons." This will
explain your tardiness and disheveled appearance, and it's
virtually impossible to disprove. Of course, with only four
tires on your car, this scenario has a limited life span, so
you'll need to mentally store up several other similarly
plausible lies. Are we having fun yet?

➢ **"Going to the gym" is a good story** but can only be used if
you actually look like you've worked out in the last fifteen
years. If your man boobs are hanging down to your beer
gut, she won't buy it. You'll also need to remember to take
your workout clothes and rub them over a sweaty
homeless guy so they look and smell appropriately rank
when you get home.

> Get adept at car sex to avoid leaving a paper trail to any local hotel, or to avoid being seen by someone who knows Wifey. I know, the last time you tried this, you threw your back out, pulled a hamstring, and narrowly missed impaling yourself on the gearshift. But she was worth it, right?

> Pick hotels that you know, with absolute certainty, no one in your social circle ever frequents. *Ever.* This reduces the possibility of anyone you know seeing you (or, God forbid, videoing you from their cell phone) with Oh-Baby, canoodling in the bar. This might require a hotel search in Botswana, but, if that's not practical, go ahead and play the odds. Maybe you'll get lucky.

> Buy a second cell phone that looks exactly like the one you already have, for calls to and from Oh-Baby, and keep it on your person at all times. Leave the old phone lying around. Even if Wifey gets suspicious, when she checks the call log or text messages, she won't find anything. "But the phone is $600," you say, "with an additional monthly fee." Stop whining. It's cheaper than the divorce settlement.

> Learn how to freeze or turn back the odometer on your car. Taking Oh-Baby to the beach for the weekend, when the beach is 500 miles away, is going to be hard to hide. Don't worry about the illegality issue. Better angry DMV workers than a betrayed spouse.

> Have a posse in place to cover for you on those inevitable nights Wifey calls looking for you while you're out doing the freaky with Oh-Baby. Be extremely careful about who you select. In many marriages, spouses tell each other everything. Posse Guy may very well tell *his* wife (of course, swearing her to secrecy). But once another

woman knows, the clock often starts ticking. Don't worry too much, though. She probably won't tell anyone else. Really, she won't.

➤ **Buy Oh-Baby the same fragrance Wifey wears.** Oh-Baby doesn't need to know, and you won't come home at midnight smelling like the tool you actually are. Ditto with lipstick. It might be difficult getting her to wear the same fragrance or lip color as Wifey, especially if they don't look anything alike and have completely different preferences. But I'm sure she'll understand. Go ahead. Ask her.

➤ **If Wifey ever becomes suspicious and confronts you, learn to deflect by pushing a hot button.** "*Seriously*? You sound *just like your mother* when you get like this." This usually sets off a big ol' nasty fight that will take her mind off of her original question. Sure, it tanks the evening, but Oh-Baby can make it all better later, right?

➤ **Make cue cards to record your lies**, and practice, practice, practice until they become "true" and you can keep them all straight. It also helps if you practice appropriate facial expressions. You'll need to be able to lie without looking shifty or guilty. Yes, this takes a *lot* of work, but it's necessary, if you don't want to trip yourself up.

➤ **Learn to sleep with one eye open.** Watch Oh-Baby carefully for signs of latent bunny-burner syndrome. Many men have had their weenies whacked off, been backed over by SUVs, or summarily shot by mistresses who eventually realized they would never become wives.

And there you have it. Hope this helps. Then again, maybe it would be simpler if you just stopped behaving like a nineteen-year-old bad-ass player and instead go kiss your wife while she still loves you.

"It takes a great deal of bravery
to stand up to our enemies,
but just as much to stand up to
our friends."

~J.K. Rowling

Friends. Sometimes They Just Need to be Tossed Out of the Boat

YOU KNOW who she is. She's that friend who's always asking you about your life and what you're doing, with an oh-so-interested, concerned expression permanently plastered across her face, as she skillfully touches on every sensitive topic in your emotional suitcase and adds running commentary that makes you feel somehow worse than before.

"And how's your Hubs? Is he still working with that twenty-year-old blonde tramp who was all over him at the Christmas party? Well, despite what everyone is saying, I'm *sure* nothing ever happened between them."

"And tell me about your daughter. Has she stopped dating that creepy guy with the tattoos and all those facial piercings? It must be so hard for you to watch her keep picking losers."

"So your mother is coming for the weekend? She must be back from her cruise with your sister. Tell me again why you weren't invited?"

One of the benefits of aging is that we reach a point in our lives when we get to choose who we spend our time with. We can be selective and let in only those people who lift us up, encourage us, make us laugh, forgive our mistakes, celebrate our

Friends. Sometimes they Just Need to be Tossed Out of the Boat

97

wins, and genuinely grieve our losses. And we do the same for them, because that's *how it works.*

Longevity in our lives, parallel office cubicles, or shared DNA are no longer deciding factors in selecting your tribe. Yes, we've been friends since junior high, or we've worked together for three years, or maybe we're family, but you're also kind of a bitch, and when I spend time with you, I always leave feeling "less." So buh-bye. And while you're headed out the door, please take these people with you:

- ❖ **The flake**. She shines at planning events. She packs our calendars with weekend wine tastings, girls' nights out, movie nights, or duo mani-pedis at the local day spa. But then you get the last-minute cancellation. Every. Single. Time. So don't hold her seat at the restaurant, because she's not coming.

- ❖ **The user**. Whenever she needs something, whether it's helping her move her furniture around or being the lookout while she stalks his new girlfriend all over town, you're the first person she calls. "Please, please, *please.* I'll owe you one" is her wheedling promise. But, somehow, she's always in a no-cell-service zone when you try to call.

- ❖ **The whiner**. This woman's life is a mess. And before the second glass of wine, you'll know every detail. Hubs is not paying attention to her, she hates her job, her kids are spoiled rotten and entitled, and her beloved shiatsu needs $1,000 surgery, so she's thinking of just putting him down, and life is just so haaaaaard. Forty-five minutes into the evening, you're ready to shoot yourself. And she hasn't asked you a question about yourself in over two years.

- ❖ **The gossip**. She knows everything about everyone. Her favorite activity is curling up on the couch with you and a bottle of wine while she narrates the evening with private, salacious detail of other people's lives. While this may have been fun the first couple of times, you begin to realize that this is all she talks about, *ever*. And remember, "Do it *with* me, do it *to* me." All that trash gossip she's sharing with you about them? Guess what she's telling them about *you*?

❖ **The drama queen**. She's happiest in the midst of a personal crisis, so she creates them wherever she goes. She's exhausting, needy, and, if you let her, she'll suck your energy until you've got nothing left. Then you're the bad guy, because "you don't care about her." *No one* can care enough. It's not humanly possible. Save yourself. Run for the nearest exit.

❖ **The expert**. She's got advice on every topic you've ever brought up. She knows what you're doing wrong with your kids, why Hubs has been less attentive lately, why your boss has been so hard on you, the best way to host your weekend dinner party, why you can't lose weight, and how to stop your dog from peeing in the house. She has all the answers, all the time, and starts every sentence with, "What you need to do is…" What I need to do is throw you out of my car. While I'm driving.

❖ **The Eeyore**, who starts every day with ears down and, "It's gonna rain." No matter how good your news is or how great the day has been, Eeyore will find a way to prick your balloon. "I just won the lottery!" "*The tax department is going to take half.*" "I just got these fabulous boots on sale for $250!" "*They had them down the street for $175.*" "I'm thinking of getting my hair cut short." "*If you don't like it, it'll take forever to grow back.*" While this can be adorable in a children's book character, it's *annoying* in an adult.

Friends. Sometimes they Just Need to be Tossed Out of the Boat

99

❖ **The bombshell**. While undeniably beautiful, she dresses to showcase every asset. Everything she wears looks like date night at the MILF Motel, and, if there's a man within a two-mile radius, she'll be working her moves. It doesn't matter if he's married, barely out of high school, or in a wheelchair. She needs constant validation of her desirability, and if her flirting with your hubs bothers you, well, you should try harder to look like her and maybe he wouldn't stray. These women were the originators of the bathroom brawl.

Most of us have met and befriended these women at some point in our lives. If we're lucky, they're now just memories. And they helped shape the fabulous friendships we have today. For that, we're grateful. But I'm still not accepting their friend requests on Facebook.

"*Always remember that you are absolutely unique.*
Just like everyone else."

~Margaret Mead

How to be Happy When Other People Are So Annoying

ASK TEN people you see on the street what they want most from life and eight of them will say, "I just want to be happy." They may or may not know exactly how they would define "happiness," but they could tell you why other people are responsible for keeping them from having it.

Our search for happiness often finds us pointing to external or future events. "I'll be happy *if* I lose twenty pounds." "I'll be happy *when* I win the lottery." "I'll be happy *after* my husband finishes the yurt in our backyard for my mother-in-law, so she can get the hell out of my kitchen."

When I meet people who seem to be permanently angry, I often wonder if they're *ever* happy, or if they wake up smiling but quickly shift gears when someone or something inevitably pisses them off during the day. The people who claim to "just want to be happy" are often the same ones who go all road rage in the supermarket, stuck behind an oblivious, elderly woman blocking the aisle while she ponders the merits of Aunt Jemima vs. Mrs. Butterworth; or they start out cheerful in the morning until they discover that Puddles, the family cat, peed on the couch again, at which point the entire family (including Puddles) dives for cover.

"Most folks are about as happy as they make up their minds to be," said Abraham Lincoln. I *love* this. Happiness is more often a *choice* than an event. You choose happiness when you:

- ❖ **Think of yourself less.** You can't be the bride at every wedding or the corpse at every funeral. Some days are just not about *you*. One of my favorite quotes is from Dr. Phil. "We'd worry less about what other people think about us if we realized how seldom they do." Boom.

- ❖ **Slow down.** We're all so conditioned to *go, go, go,* jamming two days' of errands into two hours after work. Our "downtime" is packed with projects that we can't possibly finish unless we forfeit sleep, bathing, and chocolate. We're frequently cranky and exhausted, and not only are we not happy, if we see anybody who is, we're taking them *down*. It's time to grab a book and head for the lake for the weekend. Say no to driving all over town to search for limited-edition huckleberry Eggos because your kids saw the commercial and thought they looked cool. Sit down and *relax*. Pour a large glass of iced tea and binge watch *The Voice*. You'll achieve Zen much more quickly when you discover that the world won't end and your family will survive if dinner is a frozen pizza. (Tip: This also works with wine.)

- ❖ **Learn to say "No."** Toddlers learn this word early. Refusing to do what they *don't* want to do frees them up to do the things they *do* want to do. Those tiny tots might be on to something. How can we make time for activities that make us happy when we're buried under obligations that aren't "required," but that we couldn't refuse? What's wrong with, "No, I'm not available for that"? Take a lesson from a toddler, and practice saying, "Raincheck?"

❖ **When in doubt, assume the best**. If a friend makes a comment or sends you a text that could be taken as a compliment *or* an insult, choose door #1. "I heard you finally quit smoking. Congratulations!" This *could* mean, "Yeah, right. For the 247th time. Forgive me if I don't pop the cork on the champagne quite yet." *Or* it could mean, "Great job! I knew you could do it. Let's celebrate!" Until you have concrete proof that she meant you're a loser, choose to put your party dress on. Now you're both happy.

❖ **If you can't imagine what you did to offend someone, you probably didn't.** "I called a friend today and she was totally non-chatty. She must be mad at me for something, but, for the life of me, I don't know what. But I'm not calling her back." Everybody else's life is not always about *you*. Maybe Hubby overdrew the checking account. Again. Maybe Baxter, her beloved Chi-Weenie, impregnated the award-winning toy poodle down the street and its owner is suing her dog. Maybe her ex ran off to Bora Bora with her sister. If you honestly can't pinpoint anything you've said or done to upset her, choose to believe it wasn't you. Then take her a bottle of wine and a shoulder.

❖ **Find a tribe of happy, supportive people.** The people you spend your time with have a huge influence on your attitudes. Their outlook on life, kids, marriage, money, and self-esteem will often become part of yours. Surround yourself with joyful, compassionate people who regularly remind you of the good in your life. Judgmental, whiny idiots who make you question every decision you make or who generally leave you feeling like crap every time you're together have no place in your bubble. Let them go, and, if they're reluctant, escort them to the door.

- ❖ **Don't compare yourself to others.** We see homeless people or "people from Walmart," and we secretly think, "Thank God, at least that's not me." It makes us feel slightly superior or selectively blessed. Great, until we inevitably compare ourselves to others who are "superior" or more blessed than *us*. Nineteen-year-olds making millions of dollars playing football. Questionably talented reality TV stars living in multi-million-dollar homes. The billionaire's daughter, who inherited the CEO position of a Fortune 500 company at age thirty. So, on any given day, God loves us more than a homeless person but not as much as a baby CEO? Stop that. Just... *Stop*.

- ❖ **Set aside time for fun.** All work and no play is no *fun*. Humans need fun. We need to laugh. We need to try new things and succeed. Or try them and fail gloriously. But, like sex, sometimes fun gets shoved behind bills, kids, work, the marriage, the yard, the dog, and finding out what that moldy smell in the bathroom means. So have fun. Be happy. This one *is* all about you. And it's all good.

"Seize the moment.
Remember all those women on
the Titanic
who waved off the dessert cart."

~Erma Bombeck

My Scale Mocks Me.
She Needs to Die

I HAVE A confession to make. No, it's not my unwavering love of all things red and winey. And it's not my twenty-year, auto-renewed subscription to *Star* magazine. Or even that, when I get stressed, Lucky Charms is my go-to comfort food. For all three meals. So here it is: I am a weigh-in addict. I cannot start my day until I weigh myself. Seriously. Can't even start the coffee. Skipped weigh-ins cause temporary confusion about how I feel about myself, because I don't know if I'm fat. I know: "fat" is subjective. One woman's "chubby" is another woman's dream weight. But before you decide that I'm the shallowest woman *ever*, my informal surveys of my girlfriends indicate that I'm not alone.

It seems that many of us have a weight that we've deemed our personal (and extremely private) "fat weight." The one we admit to *no one,* including our best friends. It's powerful enough to make or break our self-esteem. *Under* that number, and, yeah, we're still kind of hot. *Over* that number, and shit just got real. Instant panic ensues, resulting in a wide variety of creative, emotional, and sometimes hilarious responses.

I immediately start ransacking all my kitchen cabinets and fridge contents, tossing out every carbohydrate I spot (briefly considering doing the same with the wine, but I'm depressed, not insane). The wine stays, but I stock the kitchen with kale and vow to stop using my treadmill as a lingerie-drying rack; I fire it up on the spot, determined to actually get *on* the stupid thing to lose this freakin' weight. Preferably *today*. My usual breakfast of bacon, eggs, and a frosted cinnamon roll now becomes a toss-up between the self-congratulatory egg whites and turkey bacon, or what-the-hell-who-cares-I'm-a-big-fat-loser-anyway-gimme-the-damn-cinnamon-roll. It could go either way.

Sometime during puberty, the scale and I settled into what would become a lifelong battle of wills. Specifically, how do I persist in eating every crappy, non-nutritional, processed food product I love (paired up with its appropriate grape varietal) and keep those numbers where they belong? Every morning at 5 a.m., the scale and I get the gloves on and see who won the previous twenty-four-hour round. Had pizza for dinner and didn't gain an ounce? Take *that*, you piece of junk. Cut out all my carbs and *gained* a half pound?? Excuse me while I throw your scrap metal ass out the window, and you can spend the rest of the day in the begonias. Morning score: Scale, one; me, zip.

Over the years, my scale has attained mythic proportions, determining my self-esteem for each day on an impenetrable level that no amount of compliments or reassurance from Hubs, friends, or strangers on the street can impact. If I weigh *less* than The Number, I feel pretty confident. If I weigh *more* than The Number, I'm a hopeless pork chop, never to be attractive again. I weigh myself every single morning, no matter what. Going on vacation? I simply take my scale with me. Attending a conference? Slide it into my carry-on. My scale has become a traveling gnome. After four decades, it's seen three countries, flown from the West Coast to the East Coast (and back again), cruised to Alaska, and lazed on the lanai in Maui.

"Why do you *do* this to yourself?" Hubs repeatedly asks.

"I *have* to," I tell him. "If I don't weigh myself, how will I know if I'm fat?"

"Just go by how your clothes fit," he says, with slightly condescending male logic.

"That only works for *date clothes,*" I explain, rolling my eyes. "Yoga pants are stretchy. That's why we love them. But you wouldn't feel anything under five pounds. I'm five foot two. Five pounds would puff me up like a ballpark frank on the grill. And since menopause pretty much obliterated my metabolism, I can't lose weight on more than 200 calories a day, so *I'd stay that way forever.*"

He eventually admitted defeat, mumbling, "Next time, I'm marrying the first woman I meet who doesn't own a damn scale."

Not surprisingly, with 16,425 weigh-ins behind me at last count, I've uncovered a few tricks to help salvage what might otherwise be a bad day. Weigh-in novices, take note:

> **Pee**. Twice, if you can. Water can add up to two pounds on the scale. And people who say, "It's just water weight" are idiots. And probably skinny.

> **Get nekkid**. *Never* weigh in with your clothes on. When I threatened to strip in the doctor's waiting room hallway and the doc determined that I *was not bluffing*, she began letting me use the scale in the nurse's bathroom.

> **Find your scale's sweet spot**. There's a certain angle at which you can lean that will literally "lighten the load." Experiment. It's there. Twenty-degree tilt to the right, and I'm up to two pounds lighter. There are mornings when this *matters*.

> **Weigh yourself on the same scale whenever possible**. The scales you buy at Walmart or at your local Weight Watcher's meeting have a lot of play. Your weight can

show a three-pound variable from scale to scale. This isn't a big deal if it's three pounds *less* than you normally weigh, but three pounds more can tank a day.

I know what many of you are thinking. "What is *wrong* with this woman?? I could *never* be that vain or that superficial. Get her some help. *Now.*"

You're right. I should probably seek professional help. But it's truly not about vanity or self-absorption. I don't think the world revolves around my weight or that anyone else gives a rat's behind. But *I* do.

We can't control getting older. We can't control the effects of gravity (*Really,* God??) We can't control our hormones or our post-menopausal metabolism. I *can* control my weight. *But not unless I know what it is.*

Hubs recently brought me an article that offered a potential solution to my fixation. It suggests starting with an every-other-day weigh-in, tapering off by one per week, with the ultimate goal being no more than once a week. Behavioral modification for scale junkies. Who would've thought? After one month, I think I get a pin.

And if we ever have a meeting, I'll bring the wine.

"Bottom line is, if you do not use it or need it, it's clutter, and it needs to go."

~Charisse Ward

Downsizing. (AKA "Giving all Your Crap to Your Kids")

Check any magazine counter and you'll find shelves full of articles about downsizing. An entire generation of baby boomers is discovering the freedom of owning less and doing more. We're selling our four-bedroom family homes and buying 500-square-foot houses or condos, trading in our expensive cars (and hefty payments) for RVs to travel the countryside, and leaving the security of our 9-5 jobs to pursue our bliss, hoping we'll still be able pay for groceries next week. We realize that life is short, so, if we're ever going to live out our dreams, it has to be *now*.

For most of us, a huge part of this process is figuring what to do with all our crap. The stuff we've accumulated, purchased, collected, or received from friends and family on holidays, birthdays, and anniversaries. At one time, this stuff was important. We wore it, displayed it, drove it, lived in it, and protected it with insurance policies and alarm systems. It *defined* us and showed the world our worth. Now, the children are grown, the family dog has passed on, the credit cards are paid off, and our stuff is all that's standing between us and freedom.

Yet we're not prepared to throw it all away or give it to a second-hand store. Much of our stuff is personal. Some of it was expensive. How do we divest of our worldly goods as we transition to our tiny new houses that won't accommodate forty-five years' of *things*? And our new RV has one small closet and three drawers. Who do we give all this crap to? Who will want it and take care of it like we did?

The kids.

Yep, let's give all the tired or dated junk to Goodwill and the cool stuff to the kids. I mean, they'd be crazy not to want all this. It's way better than giving them money. This is the perfect plan. They get a big pile of seriously cool shit they don't have to buy, and we get the comfort of knowing that our prized possessions are in good and grateful hands.

Whoa. Slow down, Nellie. Before you back up the Matson shipping container onto their front yard, anticipating welcoming smiles from your delighted offspring, you might want to call ahead and ask your child (and his/her spouse) if they do, in fact, covet your collection of 127 albums from the '60s and '70s, including the slightly warped but still playable *Best of the Village People.*

Questionable crap includes:

❖ **Your gigantic, ten-year-old Nordic Track treadmill**, that takes up roughly half their spare bedroom and hasn't actually been turned on since 2009. Telling your DIL that it also makes a great clothes hanger for bras and other items she doesn't want to put in the dryer isn't going to make that behemoth any smaller or less of a pain in the ass for them, when they move.

❖ **Your commemorative State Plates collection.** Sure, Oregon has been missing since it mysteriously jumped off the wall and shattered on Halloween, 1984. And Vermont has a large, orangey glue mark running down the center where it broke in half and Hubs repaired with it Gorilla Glue. Don't ask about Louisiana. It got inexplicably lost sometime around 1992 and hasn't been seen since. Just tell the kids not to display them in alphabetical order, and no one will notice.

❖ **Grandma's silver set, for twenty**. Never mind that it has to be kept in a special box and each piece must be hand-polished before every use. Oh, and it can't ever be put in the dishwasher. Yeah, the kids will be using these daily.

❖ **Ditto for Grandma's heirloom porcelain dish set**, complete with gravy boat and soup tureen.

❖ **Your old tool set**, which has been out in your Tough Shed for thirty-plus years, is missing critical pieces, and is in desperate need of cleaning. Especially since neither your son nor his wife has ever exhibited any skill or desire to fix their cars or the wiring in their rented home.

❖ **The beat-up Chevy in your garage**, that hasn't run since 1972 but "just needs some love and attention." If you couldn't get it running, how are *they* going to?

❖ **Those fifteen boxes of photo albums**, including your high school graduation pics, your wedding photos (first and second marriages for both of you), and the approximately 2,000 pictures of your child growing up. While these albums may be interesting to your children downline at some point, usually decades later, until then, they will have to survive every move.

❖ **Your clothes**. I realize that you're RVing to warmer weather and won't need that still-serviceable plaid, flannel coat you've been wearing every winter since 1989, but he's not going to want it. And Mom's expensive, long dresses, while gorgeous on a sixty-something woman, will make your DIL look like a frumpy mother of the bride. She's twenty-four. Consider donating these to *her* mother.

Downsizing. (AKA "Giving all Your Crap to Your Kids")

117

❖ **The 182 tiny metal toy trucks** from your forty-year obsession collection. Yes, I know it took years to cultivate, and getting those last two models required six trips and four months of negotiations with the original owner. But trust me: these are not always shared passions. Avoid hurt feelings or someday stumbling across your entire collection displayed in their next garage sale for five bucks.

❖ **Your collector show car** that only gets taken out of its climate-controlled garage for parades and car shows. The kids have no place to store it and no idea how to maintain it. Nor do they have the means. This is not a gift. This is a money-sucking *project*. Give this to a rich friend.

❖ **Your books**. We grew up in the hardback-book era. Our homes boasted large bookcases, laden with best-selling authors, self-help books, travel guides, and tutorials on every recognized hobby, prominently displayed in our living rooms and home offices. Our kids grew up with Kindles. 40,000 books on one thin, 5x8" device. You can't compete. Make a librarian (and your kids) happy, and donate your books today.

Good luck. May your future be bright, and may all your junk turn out to be treasures.

"Some women (and here I'm referring to my wife) can share as many as three days' worth of feelings about an event that took eight seconds to actually happen."

~Dave Barry

Men Confess:

What They're Really Thinking When We're Talking

ONE NIGHT I was having a small pity party over something I no longer remember, and I told Hubs he didn't seem to love me as much as he used to. He did the appropriate hubby thing and gave me a hug, repeating how much he loved me and how lucky he was, blah, blah, blah, but I sensed a certain sigh in his voice and challenged him on it.

"Fine," he said and rolled his eyes. "I was actually thinking, *Are you nuts?* I just spent a week painting the entire inside of our house pink because that's what you wanted. *Pink.* I sure as hell didn't pick it. If I wasn't crazy about you, it would have been painted a *normal* color, like beige, which I won't have to completely redo when we sell the house."

Notwithstanding that it wasn't pink—it was *salmon*—he had a point.

I began to think about the vast sea of articles written about the centuries-old lament from men that women have some weird language they'll never understand and how exhausting is is constantly trying to figure out what we're thinking. But let's get real here. We don't always know what's really behind *your* responses, either.

I decided to conduct a quick survey among our married friends about their communication issues, and it resulted in the following hilarious exchanges about what the men were really thinking when their wives were talking.

She says: "You never listen to me anymore."

He says: "I'm sorry. Let me put down the remote and give you my full attention."

He's thinking: "Seriously, babe? All I *do* is listen, because you're *always* talking."

ೠೠ

She says: "You don't love me as much as you used to."

He says: "Of course I do. I love you as much today as I did the day we got married."

He's thinking: "For the love of God, woman, I just walked your stupid toy poodle, Lola, past my gym while she was wearing her tiny mink jacket. Now I have to drive across town to work out. What do you *want* from me?"

ೠೠ

She says: "I love you."

He says: "I love you too."

He's thinking: "Yippee! I'm getting laid!"

ೠೠ

She says: "Can we talk?"

He says: "Of course. Let me get some wine and I'm all yours."

He's thinking: "Oh, crap. No woman has *ever* begun a sentence with that as a segue to, 'We just won the lottery and we need to figure out what to do with the $358 million.' Ever. Whatever it is, it's *bad*."

ର୍ଷର୍ଷ

She says: "My old boyfriend just got promoted to Regional Director at Microsoft."

He says: "Good for him."

He's thinking: "Great. She's probably wishing she would've married him. I'll never make that kind of money, and she knows it. Her mother is right. I'm a loser."

ର୍ଷର୍ଷ

She says: "It was such a long day at work. Why don't you pour us some wine and get comfy while I change, and then I can tell you about it."

He says: "Sure, sweetie. Maybe a bubble bath would help? Oh, and your sister called."

He's thinking: "If I can get her sidetracked, maybe I can avoid the play-by-play of her eight-hour day with a bunch of people I don't know and don't give a crap about."

ର୍ଷର୍ଷ

She says: "Guess what today is?"

He says: "I don't have to guess, honey. I was just considering where we should go to celebrate."

He's thinking: "I'm *so* dead. If I guess and I'm wrong, I'm screwed. If I tell her I don't have a clue, I'm forever the douche husband who forgot the date we first kissed or danced together or, oh God, what else do we celebrate? Somebody help me. Anybody??"

ର୍ଷର୍ଷ

She says: "It was on sale!"

He says: "Great! And you're right, it looks expensive."

He's thinking: "It looks expensive because it *is*. And the last time you brought home something 'on sale,' it was those black boots that you got for $400 instead of $600. A *sale* is three for $10, free shipping. You have no credibility anymore, woman."

ଔଔ

She says: "Let's just call your brother to fix it."

He says: "It's just some plumbing. No worries. I got this."

He's thinking: "She obviously believes I have no freakin' clue how to fix anything around the house, so let's just call my brother, who, by the way, isn't a plumber, either, but since *he* fixed their toilet, he's the man. Bite me, bro."

ଔଔ

She says: "I'm okay. Don't worry about it."

He says: "Come here so I can give you a hug. If there's anything else I can do, just let me know."

He's thinking: "Okay, jackass, what did you do that made her cry? She's really upset, and you know it's *your fault*. Think, man. *Think. What did you do*??"

ଔଔ

She says: "Our sex life is fine."

He says: "Okay. That's good."

He's thinking: "Fine? *Fine*?? I once told her she looked 'fine,' and she burst into tears. But it's good enough to describe our sex life? So our sex life sucks. I suck at sex. Her Microsoft boyfriend was probably *great* in bed, even though he's an arrogant tool."

ଔଔ

This all gave me an idea for a new board game. It'll be called *What She Said, What He Said, What He Thinks.* Two or more couples, to make it more fun. The woman draws a card of common female statements and reads the phrase to her partner. He responds in his usual manner, and she has ten seconds to figure out what he's *really* thinking.

I'm thinking we're gonna be rich.

"Drama does not just walk into your life.
Either you create it, invite it, or associate with it."

~Unknown

How to Ditch the Drama-Mama
(Even if She's You)

I GOT A call last weekend from an obviously distressed friend, who blasted me with a thirty-minute, breathless tirade about her belief that her hubby and her best friend were having an affair. My first reaction was to make a joke, because this woman thinks every female in town is hot for her hubs and that, whenever he's "working late," he's getting his freaky on with one of her friends. To my knowledge, he's *never* cheated on her, but that doesn't seem to matter. She's always *sure*. And she's always pissed.

Every option I offered was stubbornly met with, "If I see that bitch, she's going to be sorry she messed with me and mine." Attributing her intermittent female gang-banger personality disorder to her chronic off-the-charts stress levels, I spent the next hour in a futile effort to talk her off the ledge. Unfortunately, it became apparent that was not what she wanted. She seemed to be enjoying her victim role and was milking it for all it was worth. I ended the call and, ultimately, the friendship.

Drama Mamas (aka Drama Queens) are people who overreact and get intensely upset about any small encounter or setback. Catastrophe is always about to befall them. Their lives are a constant whirlwind of disasters and conflicts, magnified into histrionic dramas plastered all over Facebook and burning up their phone lines with anyone who will listen.

One of the best things about aging is letting go of drama. We're at a time in our lives when we seek a calmer, more positive place in our daily lives and relationships. We Zen our thoughts and feng shui our living rooms. We take jobs we love instead of jobs we need. We become less judgmental. We downsize our homes, our cars, and our material needs, reducing the burden of "too much stuff." We have less, so we can do more.

Drama increases stress, ruins relationships, and sucks up time we may not have left. Drama Mamas may be longtime friends or even family members, but that doesn't make them less toxic. If you're feeling sucked into the swirling vortex of a Drama Mama's life, it might be time to clean house. If it's *you*, you just identified your new project for the next year.

Whatever the source, there are things we can do to decrease drama in our lives:

- **Don't assume the worst**. "Hubs is working late again. He must be cheating on me." "My best friend doesn't pick up when I call. She must be mad at me." Maybe Hubs just has a lot of work to do and Suzie is in the shower. It's not always a grand conspiracy about *you*.

- **When faced with two possible explanations, assume the most positive option is true**. "Hubs called my sister nine times last week. They're either having daily phone sex or planning my surprise sixtieth birthday party." Until you know otherwise, go shopping for a new party dress.

- **Believe half of what you read and none of what you're told**. Remember the Telephone Game when you were young? You all sit in a circle and, one by one, whisper the same sentence to each other around the room. The last person then says what he heard, which gets compared to what the first person actually said. Hilarity ensues when everyone hears two completely different statements. The lesson here: If a rumor has gone through more than two people, chances are you're getting a revised edition.

+ **Keep things in perspective**. Very few incidents during an average day signal the Rapture anytime soon. That guy who cut you off in traffic? Maybe he's trying to get his sick child to the hospital. Maybe his mother just had a heart attack. Maybe he's just a douche. But chances are you'll never see him again. Is it worth spending the entire evening ranting about?

+ **Walk away from gossipmongering**. It sounds juicy and can even seem kind of fun, but gossip sessions are the epicenter of dysfunction and drama. Besides, if you don't hear it, you can't repeat it. Win-win.

+ **Don't post anything anywhere online that you're not prepared for everyone *on the planet* to see**. Every day, there are horror stories about friendships and family relationships being obliterated because someone saw something on Facebook the writer thought they'd never see. Assume everything you post online will be seen by your parents, your kids, your minister, and the person you wrote it about.

+ **Be the first to say I'm sorry**. "An eye for an eye" might feel satisfying in the moment, but it won't help you eliminate petty conflicts in your life. It's not just about who's right. It's about who wants the relationship back.

+ **Pick your battles**. Is it really necessary to hurl public insults over a lost parking space or who saw that fabulous blue sweater first? Drama Mamas have trouble making distinctions between petty annoyances and true crisis situations. A snippy comment from a salesclerk elicits the same DEFCON-level response as the idiot driver who totaled her new car. Learn to differentiate, and save your emotional energy for what really matters.

🔹 **Give others the benefit of the doubt.** Maybe the woman who snapped at you in the grocery line just discovered that her husband cleaned out the marital checking account and ran off to Bora Bora with the nineteen-year-old Swedish nanny. Or the waiter who rolled his eyes at you when you asked for that third basket of bread sticks had his car repossessed that morning. If you can't think of what you did, you probably didn't. Despite what your mother told you when you were a child, the world isn't always about *you*. Let it go.

To live a more peaceful life, weed out the Drama Mamas whenever possible. If you can't eliminate them, limit contact. People don't automatically get to be part of your life simply because of shared DNA or matching sorority keys from 1989. Decide what, and who, you want in your life, and you will live more joyfully.

"Girls do not dress for boys.
They dress for themselves and
each other.
If girls dressed for boys,
they'd just walk around naked at
all times."

~Betsey Johnson

Frumpy Fashion.
What Not to Have in Your Closet at Any Age

GOOGLE "What Not to Wear After 50" or "Fashion Dos and Don'ts After Menopause," and you'll find a tsunami of advice articles. From *Time* magazine's commentary on current fashion trends to Tina Fey's stand-up comedy, it seems everyone (including, I confess, me) has an opinion on what works and what doesn't after any given decade. Trendy choices at twenty often look unsophisticated at thirty. What works at thirty may look cougar-ish at forty. And what was flattering at forty can look downright slutty at fifty.

But there are certain things that don't work well on any woman old enough to have a knee-jerk reaction when being referred to as a "girl" by her male boss. It's not about chronological age. It's about arriving at a time in your life when you want to be seen as a strong, intelligent, grown-up woman with something valuable to offer, and who's not afraid to be *seen*. It's about tossing clothes that make you fade away. Clothes that make you invisible.

Whatever your age (and whatever your weight), it might be time to ransack your closet and toss the following:

➢ **Oversize items or maternity wear to hide your weight.** Nothing you can buy at Hilo Hattie's House of Muumuus has ever made a woman look smaller. No matter what your actual size might be, shrouding your body from head to toe in a pup tent says, "I'm fat, but I'm hoping you won't notice."

➢ **Tiny, old-lady, floral fabrics.** Nothing screams "old lady in the background" like tiny floral prints that channel Grandma Bertha's kitchen wallpaper in the old farmhouse.

➢ **Mid-calf skirt or dress lengths.** Unless you're a gazelle with mile-long legs, skirts that hit you at the widest part of your calves will make you look shorter and chunkier (read: *frumpier*). Assuming this isn't the look you're going for, hem them slightly above or slightly below the kneecap.

➢ **Ugly shoes.** Boxy, clunky footwear. Yes, there comes that sad, sad day when we must relinquish our stilettos and consider shoe styles that don't aggravate our sciatica, that allow us to cross the room without toppling over or spraining an ankle, and that don't make us cranky all day because our feet are throbbing. Thankfully, there are now entire stores devoted to fabulous, comfortable flats and low heels.

➢ **Bad bras.** Ill-fitting bras that don't get those puppies back *up there* can make you look dumpy and frumpy. Remember Great-Aunt Hilda, from your childhood? She had a "funny body," her boobs hung down to her waist, and she was *old* (definitely in her fifties).

➢ **Self-belts.** Those tiny little belts that come with the dress or the jeans? Remove them. Preferably at the sales counter. High-quality statement belts do not come as a gift-with-purchase. The ones that match the dress or add a little bling to the jeans are predictable and cheaply made, and they look it.

> **Peter Pan collars**. *Especially* if they're lace. On dresses, blouses, or any other item of clothing, if you're over the age of nine. They make you look like an Amish schoolteacher. Which is great if you're actually an Amish schoolteacher. But, otherwise, a little too "sweet."

> **Cheap grandma purses** made from vinyl or "pleather." Usually beige or black, with an adjustable shoulder strap and *lots* of compartments, so you don't lose your reading glasses, car keys, or wadded stash of grocery coupons.

> **Sweatpants with elastic ankles**. Invented by a misogynistic eunuch who thinks women should look invisible and sexless. Nailed it. These do not make us look like Jeannie from *I Dream of...* They're the quintessential "I don't care, and I'm not actually here" piece. The yoga pants of rural matrons.

> **Elastic waistbands**. Worn nationwide by middle-aged women who say they're *comfortable*. But bunching a yard of fabric around your waist acts like a life-size hair scrunchie. The only thing less flattering than a fanny pack (see #16).

> **Ruffles**. There comes a time (no later than thirty) when ruffles down the front of a blouse or around the collar leaves behind "girlish" or "feminine" and becomes fifty-year-old Church Lady.

> **Lace**. See Ruffles. And too much of it can make you look like a human doily. Hard to be taken seriously when you look like you should be draped over the armrest of Great-aunt Agnes's couch.

> **Mom jeans**. High-waisted, pegged legs, medium-blue wash, in heavy denim with pockets that add ten pounds to your waistline. If they're available at a "Mart" and you paid less than $20, you've found them.

> **Mom jeans with white sneakers**. Nothing screams "I just want to blend in" quite like this combination. Throw in a boxy, oversize top and mall hair, and you've nailed it.

> **Heavy pantyhose in "Nude" or "Skintone."** I've never seen real skin in those colors. If you must wear nude pantyhose, go to a store for a brand that offers more than light, beige, or Oompa-Loompa suntan, and doesn't come in a plastic egg or a baggie.

> **Fanny packs**. Yep, get all dressed and cute, and then slap a large pouch of tent fabric around your hips. Very "country tourist in the big city." And almost anything will perform the same function without looking like your ass has grown a goiter.

> **Square cable-knit sweaters**. Great-grandma Moses. Are these still around? Excluding the "Ugliest Christmas Sweater" contest at your office (and understanding that these are unflattering and frumpy *before* you bedazzle them with light-up rhinestone Christmas trees), these should be given away immediately. To someone you don't like.

> **Matchy-matchy**. Bags and shoes that match. Sweater sets. Eyeshadow and clothing. It's dated and uninspired. Shake it up a little. And have fun!

"*I saw that.*"

~Karma

Karma Called.
She Wants to Talk to You

WHEN ASKED about the definition of "Karma," most people would say it means, "You get what you give," or "You get what you deserve." And, of course, the ever-popular, "Karma's only a bitch if you are."

The idea of getting back what you give is a familiar theme, but covers only the *first* of the Twelve Laws of Karma. Newton said, "For every action, there is a reaction." That's Karma. Every thought, word, or action we send out into the universe reflects back onto us in like fashion.

Some people say that the Laws of Karma are a bit mystifying. All that talk about higher consciousness, positive intentions, and universal connections: great for philosophical debate, but not readily translatable into our daily lives. Zen guides offer gentle, "Let's all play nice and learn to love each other" explanations, but I prefer the grassroots, "Knock that crap off and be a decent person" approach.

The Great Law (aka The Law of Cause and Effect). If you're a douche husband who cheats on his wife, if you take credit for the good things someone else did, or if you don't sign up for an annual membership to the ASPCA after watching their TV commercial with Sarah McLachlan's "Angel" playing in the background, you're going to come back as a mushroom in somebody's back yard. And they'll own a tractor mower.

The Law of Creation. If you can't figure out why you're always surrounded by drama, stress, and idiots, it's more likely created by something *you* are doing that needs to be addressed before you start working on the apparent stupidity of mankind. We call this, "Pick the weeds out of your own garden before you start tending to mine."

The Law of Humility. If you're repeatedly accused of being condescending, entitled, self-absorbed, judgmental, or selfish (or just a total tool when you're drunk, which is, unfortunately, not an infrequent occurrence), spend your energies working on *that*. It'll keep you busy for years.

The Law of Growth. If you believe that the purpose of life is to have lots of money, fame, or power and you're willing to do *whatever it takes* to make that happen, you might get it, but Karma will come to the party (usually when you least expect it) and bite you on your narcissistic ass.

The Law of Responsibility. Our parents used to say, "You made your bed. Now lie in it." Boom. Your four divorces are not entirely the fault of your money-grubbing ex-wives. Your bankruptcy wasn't caused by someone hacking into your checking account. If you never had time for your children while they were growing up, don't get pissy when they don't have time for you when you're old and lonely.

The Law of Connection. Karma has a long memory. If you think Karma "forgot" that you've been a horrible husband, a disloyal friend, or a stingy employer in the past and that your future is guaranteed to be all unicorns and glitter because you're just, well, *so awesome*, take time in the present to watch *A Christmas Carol*. Ebenezer Scrooge thought he was all that, too.

The Law of Focus. You hear that an office co-worker recently bought an expensive house by the lake. Your sister has a designer wardrobe that you covet *bad*. Your BFF was able to quit her day job and start a mink farm because she's married to a neurosurgeon who makes a gazillion dollars a year. *Your* hubs is a plumber, so no mink farm for you. Everyone seems to have more than you, and that's all you think about. But if you're busy focusing on what you *lack*, supply has no room in your life.

The Law of Abundance. Whether your abundance comes from love, friendship, talents, or money, if you're unwilling to give back to the universe or to the people who helped you get there (you didn't really think you achieved this all by yourself, did you?), the only people at your funeral will be six homeless guys trolling for the free buffet.

The Law of Here and Now. If you're spending all your days in the past, reliving your glory days when you were young, hot, and didn't have a mortgage, a struggling career, or a boomerang kid who's moved back home "just until he can save some money" (he's been in the guest room for four years now), you're missing the present moment. If you're constantly worried about your future (Will I be healthy? Will I be happy? Will I still be married to this jackass?), you're missing the present moment. Carpe diem, people.

The Law of Change. If you're can't find a "good man" because you keep dating losers with gambling or substance addictions, it's not what *they're* doing that isn't working for you. It's what *you're* doing. Raise your bar and date the kind of man you want to be with. Your experiences will only change if you do.

The Law of Patience. You see a luxury car you love but can't afford. You buy it anyway. Six months later, the thrill has worn off and you still have fifty-four payments to make.

You want to lose ten pounds, but eating better and exercising take too long, so you hit the drugstore for some "natural" speed that promises to "reduce your appetite and give you lots of energy." You lose the weight but haven't slept for a week and you're bitchy *all the time*. This morning, your family left for Hawaii without you.

You want to be married, but you're not in love with the guy you're dating. He's persistent, and you don't want to wait any longer, so you give in. But while you were planning your wedding to a guy you don't love, your cosmic soul mate began frequenting your favorite Starbucks. He's now engaged to the barista.

The Law of Gratitude. If you have a car to drive, a job, food to eat, family and friends who love you, and you aren't living in a shelter, schlepping all your worldly goods around in a shopping cart you boosted from Safeway, stop whining. Many people can't be happy because they're not grateful for what's in front of them. They're too busy wishing for *more*. If you're not grateful for what you've been given, Karma has no problem taking it back and giving to someone who will be.

Namaste.

"Sex without love is a meaningless experience, but as far as meaningless experiences go, it's pretty damn good."

~Woody Allen

Sex. The Good, The Bad, And the What the Hell Were We Thinking??

SEX. WE think about it, talk about it, chase it, avoid it, admit to it, deny it, yearn for it, or may be content without it. Some women believe it's second only to chocolate, while others, frankly, don't understand what the fuss is all about.

But it weaves itself into our lives consistent with wherever we're at, at that moment. Sex at twenty is not the same as sex at fifty. Married sex is different than dating sex. Sex evolves as our lives and relationships change.

This got me thinking about the different types of sex we have as we grow up and grow older, and I found myself laughing out loud at my own mental snapshots of various sexual experiences. I am sure many of us can relate: some were good, some questionable, and some could only be classified as "What the *hell* were we thinking??"

- ♋ **Virginity sex**. May or may not be precipitated by a riotous game of beer pong or tequila shooters boosted from Mom and Dad's alcohol cupboard.

Sex. The Good, the Bad, and the What the Hell Were We Thinking?

147

The good: Drunk young pups can still perform (although arguably well, which won't matter because she has nothing to compare it to). It's exciting and "forbidden" and chock-full of wondrous discoveries about our bodies and what those little endorphins we read about in health class are capable of.

The bad: We're young and inexperienced. We haven't done it enough to be good at it, and we are really not comfortable asking for anything we want. (And how the hell would we know, anyway?) At this age, we're long on enthusiasm but short on technique.

✆ **Dating sex.** Commonly referred to as "casual sex." Often occurs after an evening out with someone you really like but don't necessarily see as a life partner. Also described as "friends with benefits" or "hooking up."

The good: It can be fun and temporarily satisfying without requiring much emotional investment. Either party is free to walk away without the messy damage control often necessary in an actual break-up.

The bad: Often, only one of you is thinking of this as casual. The other is privately doe-eyed and waiting for you to wake up and realize the two of you are destined to be together forever. Many long-term friendships have tanked when the truth finally got blurted out during after-glow pillow talk.

✆ **Walk of Shame Sex.** Recognized by repeatedly banging your head into the shower wall the next morning, wailing "Oh my God, oh my God. What the hell was I *thinking*??" This includes one-night stands, office affairs, or sex with married politicians.

The good: Since this behavior is frequently alcohol-induced, you can claim no memory of propositioning your sister's fiancé before passing out on his couch, or that your pink thong panties have been AWOL since 10:00 last night. Amnesia can provide plausible deniability.

The bad: If you have to ask... As my mother would say, "It's not your best presentation, dear." If too many apple martinis tend to make your clothes fall off, consider not having that third one the next time you go out. Nobody ever regretted *not* doing this.

♋ **Phase 1 sex**. Otherwise known as "falling in love."

The good: *Everything.*

The bad: Thinking... thinking... thinking... Nope, I've got nothing.

♋ **Married sex**.

The good: You *know* each other. He knows exactly what spot makes your left foot thump like a happy puppy. You know which piece of lingerie makes his pupils dilate. You have a sexual dance, and, if necessary, it can get you both zinging in less time than it takes for the guests to notice you're not at the table.

The bad: Like any activity, if repeated over a long period of time in exactly the same way, it can become routine, predictable. Being naked at the same time is no longer automatically considered foreplay. ("We just did that last week. I'm good." "Me too. Besides, your parents are on their way over and you still need to make the clam dip.") Married sex can stay exciting, but at least one of you is going to need to get creative.

Sex. The Good, the Bad, and the What the Hell Were We Thinking?

149

∅ **Ex sex**. This includes sex with your ex-spouse, ex-boyfriend from college, or ex-high school flame during your class reunion weekend.

The good: Since you probably didn't plan ahead for this, it's spontaneous and "in the moment," temporarily erasing all memories of why you two didn't work the first time, focusing purely on whatever sexual chemistry brought you together "way back when."

The bad: Can be disastrous if either of you is currently in a new relationship. But, even single, it often results in a three-day binge on Ben & Jerry's Cookie Dough Delight while trying to figure what, if anything, it meant. I've *never* met a woman who slept with an ex and then remarked the next morning, "Best idea *ever*. I should have done that sooner."

∅ **Forbidden sex**. Otherwise known as "cheating."

The good: Are you seriously waiting for something here?

The bad: Pretty much everything. Actually, correct that. *Absolutely* everything.

∅ **Makeup sex**. Often occurs after a fight. Sometimes after cheating sex (but I wouldn't count on it).

The good: Can be intense and more like it "used to be" when you were first in love and couldn't get enough of each other.

The bad: At some point, you're going to have to put your clothes back on and work out your problems. It might simply be a marital blip ("If you loved me, you'd remember to put the damn toilet seat down") or the result of a spectacularly stupid decision (see #7 above), but makeup sex just puts fires on the back burner. It doesn't put them out.

And so it seems that sex is a part of *life*. It's usually good but occasionally leaves us wondering why we didn't just stay home and read a book. But, deep down, we know why. Because, when it's good, it can rock your world.

Sex. The Good, the Bad, and the What the Hell Were We Thinking?

151

"I'm in the public eye, so I don't care who knows what I get done.
If I see something sagging, dragging, or bagging,
I get it sucked, tucked, or plucked."

~Dolly Parton

Cosmetic Surgery. Would You Do It?
Would You Admit It?

Cruising Facebook the other day, I saw a post from a woman who announced to 7,000 of her closest friends that she'd just returned from a third stint at Serenity Lane and was now determined to remain "clean and dry." It seemed this was quite a bombshell, because the resulting thread expressed the high shock of friends (and future employers) around the country who'd had no clue she had a drinking problem. They do now.

I got to thinking about how much personal information we put out on social media. We post about our successes (or failures) at rehab, our mental health issues, struggles with spouses, boomerang kids, crazy exs, certifiable families, horrible bosses, and our colonoscopy results. Details we used to discuss only in late-night, wine-induced confessions to our BFFs are now blasted out every morning to the universe before our first cup of coffee.

But in all this oversharing, it occurred to me that I've never read any posts about someone having had any recent nip/tucks. Apparently, we'd rather admit to a secret OxyContin stash in our underwear drawer than share the fact that we recently had our belly fat sucked out or got our eyes "done." Cosmetic intervention has become the last taboo.

The American Society for Aesthetic and Plastic Surgery (ASAPS) reports that we spend $11 billion a year in the U.S. on cosmetic procedures. Yep, eleven billion dollars on something that nobody's doing. Well, *somebody's* doing it.

There are telltale signs. If you see a woman over forty with a smooth, unlined forehead that doesn't move when she talks, she's been Botoxed. If she's a size 2 with double-D cha-chas and she resembles an upside-down Weeble, she's had them resized. If she had an unfortunate honker nose at your high school prom, but, at the twenty-fifth class reunion, it was slender and proportionate to her face, it didn't just "get better with age."

We may or may not we choose to confess our collective vanity, but the ASAPS performed over *15 million procedures* last year. I love that the number one reason cited was not "looking younger." It was, "I want to look as good as I feel." Boom. We don't *want* to look twenty-five. We don't mind looking sixty. We just don't like looking sixty and *tired*.

If you're considering getting a little outside help to lift, tighten, or smooth what middle age, menopause, and gravity have assaulted, here are a few of the most popular options:

❖ **Breast augmentation**. Commonly known as a "boob job." The doc cuts under your boob and inserts a silicone bag beneath the tissue. It is kind of like wearing a permanent, padded push-up bra. Great if you're a Victoria's Secret model and need visible boobs to get work but have the body fat of a swizzle stick. Unfortunately, this can result in loss of nipple sensation (I don't know about you, but, at sixty years of age, what else are they *for*?), hardening, or bursting inside your body and spraying internal organs with implant solution. Your other option is just to get a better bra.

❖ **Liposuction**. Sucks out excess fat from the back, belly, or thighs. Works like a human Space Saver bag to shrink fatty body parts by sucking out the fat. Sounds reasonable. But be careful. Fat in your body has to go *somewhere*. If you Hoover it out of one area, it'll show up somewhere else. I've seen many women after liposuction with beautifully flat bellies who then grew giant thighs, when the fat in their diets found a new home. I have eight pairs of Spanx instead. Much cheaper.

❖ **Botox**. The most common non-surgical procedure. Tiny injections target specific muscles in your face (frown lines, laugh lines) and temporarily "freeze" them. Your skin looks smoother and less weathered. Works beautifully, if your practitioner is experienced. This is *not* the time to bargain-hunt. Try to avoid a provider who's fresh out of Botox school and "needs the practice," or who took a three-hour class at the local Red Lion last month.

❖ **Blepharoplasty**. Aka: "Getting your eyes done." Small incisions around the upper and lower eyelids to remove fatty deposits or excess skin that make your eyes look droopy and puffy. Make sure you ask to look "more rested," not permanently stunned. You need to be able to blink. Again, get someone who's done several thousand. Successfully. This one is hard to fix if some Doogie Howser doctor screws it up. I had mine done by a board-certified, well-recognized cosmetic surgeon when I turned fifty. Still love it.

❖ **Breast lift**. This one I understand. By the time you're sixty, those perky peaches have shifted downward like underground fault lines. Your bras have gone from wispy, "Hey, Sailor" pieces of lace to full-coverage granny bras with Kevlar underwires, just to get the girls back *up there*. I did have a consult with a doctor on this one, but I opted out. (Find out why in my book, *Who Left the Cork Out of My Lunch?*)

❖ **Butt augmentation**. This one *totally* eludes me. I've spent most of my life trying to make my butt smaller, and now, women across the country are lining up, requesting Kim Kardashian's backside? I figure, until I have Ms. Kardashian's face, I don't want her butt. I'd just look like me with a gigantic ass.

❖ **Lip augmentation**. WTH?? The positive side of this one is... Nope, I've got nothing. While I get the fantasy of having lips look slightly swollen and just kissed hard, I'd prefer to wait until that actually happened. Otherwise you look like you've recently face-planted into a wasp's nest. Plus, your lips don't move properly (how could they?), causing you to appear to suffer from Bell's palsy or a recent stroke. Kissing them fuller is so much more fun.

So, with fifteen million procedures having been performed last year alone, we can safely assume that many of us have had a little something done by the time we're sixty. It's time to stop making our friends feel like God obviously loves us more than He loves them, because He gave *us* permanently perky breasts, while *they* got wet sock puppets on a clothesline. 'Fess up, ladies, and let's exchange the names of our doctors.

"Adding sound to movies
would be like
putting lipstick on
the Venus de Milo."

~Mary Pickford

Hubs Meets Technology
(Not) Love at First Sight

MY HUBS is a vintage guy. He loves all things retro. If I let him select furnishings for the house, you would reasonably assume Judy Jetson was his decorator. He likes '69 Mustangs, turntables for his albums, cassette players for his tapes, and he'd turn our kitchen into a '50s diner if I left town for more than a day.

He also likes to listen to books on tape (preferably cassettes), and "mix tapes" that he painstakingly recorded years ago from his frat-house-worthy album collection. My enthusiastic efforts to introduce him to Kindle audio books or an iPod for his music have been met with eye-rolling and deep sighs (okay, whines) of, "*Noooo,* I'm not spending that much time on the computer. It's okay for you, because *you* like computers. *I* don't."

Don't even get him started on the whole cell phone thing. Those, he will tell you, were created by Satan to destroy an entire generation's ability to communicate in real life, children who apparently believe that "you're" and "your" are interchangeable and both spelled U-R. When I showed him what the iPhone can do, he announced, in no uncertain terms, he'd rather swap his already-archaic flip phone for a Jitterbug.

"I don't *want* to take pictures, text-speak to my friends, or play music from my *phone*. And no self-respecting guy would ask his *phone* for directions. I just want to make a damn call."

Then, one day, he came home from work, all bummed and frustrated, because his boom box finally went on the fritz and started eating his favorite tapes (for those of you born after 1980, ask your parents), leaving him without music on the construction site. Here was my chance. *Nobody* sells boom boxes or cassettes anymore. If he wanted to hear books or music at work, he was going to have to embrace technology. Welcome to a new era, baby.

The next morning, I handed him my Kindle.

"What's this?" he growled.

"It's an eReader from Amazon. It's called a Kindle."

"An *eReader*?" he replied, "That's a stupid name. Sounds like eColi. Don't want it." He handed it back to me and started out the door.

"Trust me," I smiled, "It's got *books* on it." Now I had his attention.

"Whole books?" he asked, "On that little thing?"

"You'll be a veritable public library," I assured him. I showed him how to turn it on, pick a title from my list, and adjust the volume, then headed him out the door to work.

A couple of hours later, I got a call. *"What the hell are you listening to, woman??* Joe picked *50 Shades of Grey.* His wife told him it was *suspense.* Well, it's *not.* It's PORN. Three guys called their wives all confused, and one went home for the day. *We want some answers."*

Hmmm. Seems it's not so funny when *we* do it, is it? (Probably not a good time to tell him it's a series. And a movie.) I told him that the first rule of technology is, "Them who owns the device selects the contents." In other words, my Kindle, my books; your Kindle, your books.

He agreed to buy his own, if I'd help with the downloads. Done.

One down, two to go.

The next day, I gently tried to introduce the iPod. "It's got 1,000 songs it," I said.

"I don't *know* a thousand songs," he replied. "And who the hell needs 1000 songs??"

I clicked on iTunes and showed him how easy it would be for him to make a playlist of his own. My demonstration just solidified his aversion to technology. Hubs was decidedly unimpressed with the whole iTunes scroll-select-download-playlist process.

"All those stupid passwords and song selections take too long," he said, "and there's too many choices. I've got shit to *do*. I'll just borrow yours."

Oh, this was going to be interesting.

Hubs is into AC/DC, Thin Lizzy, Bruce Springsteen, and somebody called Meatloaf. My iPod Faves playlist is 976 songs by Elvis, Lesley Gore, Toby Keith, and Tom Jones. My idea of classic rock is the Eagles' guitar riff on "Hotel California." Nevertheless, I handed him my neon-pink iPod and Bose portable docking station and watched him drive off, back to the job site, ready to fire it up.

A short while later, there's The Call.

"*Seriously*??" he said. "'What's New Pussycat?' Where do you *get* this stuff?!"

Laugh all you want, buddy, but I can hear the entire crew singing boisterously in the background on the "Whoa-whoa-whoa-whoa" parts. *Somebody's* liking it. But then came "Achy Breaky Heart," by Billy Ray Cyrus, and he admitted defeat.

"I'm coming home, and we're going to get me that eColi thing that plays books and my own i-whatever-you-call-it, so I can listen to music that won't make me the laughingstock of entire construction industry." (Big sigh here) "And will you show me again how your dumb phone works? I'm probably going to need one of those, too."

Wait 'til he finds out about apps.

"Women aren't confusing. They're a Sudoku-Jenga puzzle surrounded by Rubik's cubes strapped to a terrorist screaming at you in another language."

~Mike Vanatta

How to Talk to Your Husband

Without Making Him Crazy

Those of you who follow my blog know that Hubs has never read it. Not one post. When people appear surprised, he just says that, first of all, he already knows what it's about because he was probably there when the story happened. And, secondly, he really doesn't *need* to read it because everyone he runs into in our small town tells him what I wrote about him that week. Apparently, although Hubs doesn't read my blog, many of his friends do. (Thanks, guys!)

A few weeks ago, we were chatting over a glass (okay, a bottle; don't judge) of lovely red wine at one of our favorite wine bars when a group of Hubs's male buddies spotted us and promptly pulled up chairs to join in. An hour or so later, as the group got more boisterous, someone mentioned my blog and the fact that I never give the male species equal coverage. They complained that my posts always seem to be directed at what their *wives* want from *them*. How the husbands need to step up, figure it out, and "get it right." Soon, the men were all chiming in with, "*What about us*? How about things *she* needs to know?" Never being one to back down from a writing challenge, I agreed to give them their own post. After a raucous debate that ended with a democratic vote on topics, this was the winner.

10 Things Your Husband Doesn't Want to Hear:

1. **"Notice anything different, Sweetie?"** This is a landmine for men. They *do* notice you, but it's usually more as a "package deal." Men rarely see the details like we do. A girlfriend would instantly exclaim, *"Fabulous* bag. Is it new?"* Most men would only notice a new handbag if you came out of the shower, naked and soaking wet, wearing nothing but the bag. (I had a girlfriend who did this with a pair of wildly expensive boots. Her hubby immediately called the store and ordered the other two colors. I love this woman.)

2. **"Do you know what today is?"** (Insert loud group groan at this one.) "You're killing us with this one," one guy moaned. They *want* to know "what today is." They really do. But we tend to celebrate all things big and small, while men feel like they've nailed it if they remember your anniversary. If this is five years since your first kiss or two years from the date he brought home Sir Binky, your beloved Chi-Weenie, he won't get it right. Wailing, "How could you not *remember*??" makes him feel like a schmuck and sucks any possibility of celebratory sex out of the picture. If it's a special day, *tell him* and get on to the fun part.

3. **"I only told a couple of girlfriends. They won't tell anybody."** Well, if *you* couldn't keep his ED a secret, why do you think *they* can?

4. **"I love you, Pookie Bear."** Or, God forbid, **"Can Sammy come out and play?"** (wink, wink) In public. Pet names for each other or for intimate southern regions are common, but best used *in private*. His fishing buddies will be calling him "Pookie Bear" for the rest of his life. Or forever refer to any man's junk as "Sammy." And he'll have *you* to

thank for it. "Snuggle Bunny" him all you want. But do it at home.

5. **"If I died, would you get married again?"** Well, that depends. Are you dead at fifty-two or ninety-seven? This is a stupid question, to which there is no right answer. "No" is probably not true, if she dies at fifty. "Yes" is worse, because now she thinks you're waiting for her to kick it so you can run off with her best friend, Roxie. Either answer is going to get him summarily launched out of the marital bed for the next twenty-four hours. And *he knows it*.

6. **"Do I look fat in this dress?"** The classic, all-time winner for things men don't want to hear. Seriously, what are his options? There's only one possible response, if he wants to live: "No, you look great." If you know that's what he's going to say, no matter what he actually *thinks*, why even ask?

7. **"Do you think Sally is pretty?"** Or you could just drive a tank through your living room: there'd be less damage. You wouldn't ask if you didn't think he did. So, when he says, "No," you'll say he's lying. If he says, "Yes," he's pretty much screwed. And what difference does it make if he finds Sally pretty? He's married to *you*. So, unless he is sleeping with her, who cares?

8. **"Is that what you're wearing?"** If you want to fight all night at the party, start here. It's commonly argued that women dress to impress and men dress for comfort. But this is an "equal-gender response" question. When you imply that he looks like crap, he's going to react exactly the same way *you* would if he asked you the same question on the way out the door.

9. **"Oh, you're having another drink?"** In the history of the universe, this question has never made *anyone* drink less. Especially if you ask him in a public setting. Now he feels like a three-year-old whose mommy is counting his mistakes in front of his friends. It's belittling, embarrassing, and it *doesn't work*. If you're having a problem with his alcohol intake that night, be the DD or take a cab home, and duke it out between just the two of you.

10. **"Our sex life is fine**." Ouch. "Fine" is a word you use when picking out carpet or selecting a dog groomer. "Fine" means it's okay, it'll do, we can work with it. You know that deflated feeling you get when you spend two hours getting ready and he says, "You look fine"? You just said that about his skills under the sheets. It may be awhile before you have "fine sex" again.

So, gentlemen, there you go. I promise not to forget you next time.

"Nothing ruins the flow of conversation more quickly than refusing a compliment you have just received. Never disagree with something nice that is said to you or about you."

~Letitia Baldrige

How to Compliment Other Women
(And Why You Should)

LAST WEEK, I was with a girlfriend at our favorite wine-tasting room, where we were sipping and chatting our way through a few local varietals. An hour or so into the evening, the female wine steward came up to our table and said with a smile, "I just wanted to tell you that you have really beautiful skin." I was delighted by her spontaneous and genuine compliment. It made my day.

When I got home, I happily repeated her comment to Hubs. "I tell you that all the time," he said. "You're not that excited when *I* say it."

"That's true," I replied. "But we're married. You're legally *required* to say it. And it usually constitutes foreplay, so it doesn't count. *She* had no agenda. She just thought I had great skin."

Hubs furrowed his brow, which he does whenever he's slightly confused by my logic, and went back to watching the Big Game. But it got me thinking about women and compliments. Why is it that a compliment from another woman makes us so giddy inside? And why don't we do it more often?

My completely unscientific theory is that society teaches women to be slightly competitive with each other. It's widely recognized in the retail industry that insecurities are a salesperson's unicorns and glitter. Women learn early to measure ourselves against other women, especially if the other woman is beautiful. "Wow, she looks great. I wish I looked like that."

Whether she's thinner, more fashionable, or simply appears more confident, it can make us feel like she's somehow "better." We feel weird about walking up to her and asking her where she got those fabulous boots. She's a bit intimidating, and we're not sure how she'll react. What if she's annoyed or unfriendly? Yeah, *that* would be awkward. So we stay silent and swallow our envy, hoping it will pass (or, if we're being brutally honest, that she'll suddenly develop a thyroid condition and gain twenty pounds).

So, in the spirit of female solidarity, my belated New Year's resolution (yes, in April; I'm slow, but I eventually get there) is to give a sincere compliment to one different woman every day for two weeks. I'm intrigued by the idea and curious to see the responses. It might be a good friend, an acquaintance, a co-worker, a family member, or a total stranger (those get the best reactions). If you'd like to join me, here are a few to get us started.

"You're beautiful." I've never met a woman who was offended by being told she's beautiful. Especially from someone who isn't trying to do her. (Unless you are, in which case it doesn't count.)

"*Gorgeous* handbag." This also works for shoes, boots, or any item of clothing. And haircuts. One time, a woman walked all the way across a restaurant to ask me where I bought my handbag, because she "just had to have it." That was five years ago, and I still carry that bag because she loved it so much.

"You have a great smile." Think Julia Roberts in *Pretty Woman*. Virtually every tabloid or magazine article about her mentions her mega-watt smile. It appears to come from her core, and it defines her. We covet that smile. Tell a woman she's got one, and she'll be flashing it for days.

"**Have you lost weight?**" A universal favorite for women of all ages. Be careful not to wax on with, "You look *amazing*. Wow. What a *difference*." The original compliment gets instantly obliterated when she hears, basically, that she looked like crap before. If she ever gains the weight back, she'll be suicidal. If you must keep talking, a simple, "You look great, but then you always do," is the perfect add-on.

"**You're *uber*-talented**." You may be referring to her corporate negotiating skills, her decorating skills, or her ability to make hairless cats look pretty. Everyone likes to feel special or unique in some way. (And, if she's a writer, she'll love you for life. Just sayin'.)

"**You're always so funny**." Whether she's a stand-up comedienne or just has a sharp wit with one-liners, funny people love to be told they make you laugh. Nobody stands alone in the forest and cracks jokes. Funny people thrive on audiences they can entertain. If she entertains you, tell her. You'll make her day.

"**Your kids are so smart**." "Well-behaved" is also a good one. Those two compliments will zip-line you right up to the top of her "I love you, too" list. It's women-speak for, "You're a good mother" and pretty much guarantees you a spot on her list of "People I Would Throw Myself in Front of a Bus For."

"**You're amazing just the way you are**." In a world where women often don't feel "good enough" about everything from career achievements to parenting skills or our bodies, it's a relief to hear that someone thinks we rock, right now, exactly the way we are. It tells us we can shelve our *How to Become a Better Person in Six Short Months* self-help book (at least for a couple of weeks) and get to that 400-page romance saga we've been itching to curl up with for months.

"**You look so young**." In our youth-oriented society, this is the Mac Daddy compliment. In all the years I've said this to women I've met, no one has ever responded with "Bite me." It always leans more towards "Thank you!" with a *purrrrr* and a huge smile. She'll buy the next round. Every time.

"**You are** *fabulous*." I saved this one for last because you should say it to *yourself* every morning, when you look in the mirror. That woman looking back at you is the person from whom you get the most feedback about your worth. Be as generous to yourself as you might be to another woman that day. She *is* fabulous. And so are you.

"Age is just a number. It's totally irrelevant unless,
of course, you happen to be a bottle of wine."

~Joan Collins

Sorry, But I Don't Spit

HUBS AND I live in a beautiful, small Oregon town that is becoming known for its growing number of yummy wineries. As lovers of all things red and winey, we like to reserve Thursday evenings for our personal local winery tours, checking out tasting rooms around the valley.

This time, we decided to drive up towards Mt. Hood to visit a popular winery we hadn't tried before: quaint old Victorian house with gorgeous landscaping and a majestic view of the mountain. Happily settling in, we were handed an extensive menu by the smiling young wine steward who seemed eager to describe the glowing attributes of anything we pointed to. As we were making our choices, I asked him how people manage wine tours without becoming a driving hazard. He pointed to a metal bowl on the counter and replied, "You're supposed to sip, swish, but then spit it out."

Say whut?

ARE YOU NUTS?!?

First of all, public (and communal) spitting receptacles are just *nasty*. Secondly, I was raised with three older brothers, so I've seen enough group hawking to last two lifetimes. And *thirdly*, the swish-and-spit thing is slightly reminiscent of a dental cleaning.

Not to mention, while I'm swishing, you're waxing on about the "beautiful ambiance, complex bouquet, and rich robustness with just a hint of chocolate raspberry" of the fabulous wine that I'm *not supposed to swallow*?? Say hello to the point of wine drinking, you insolent pup.

(Dear Winery, *This* is what happens when you hire twenty-two-year-old beer-pong enthusiasts to tend your wine bar.)

I was just gearing up to ask young Edwardo when the last time was *he* spit out his Pabst Blue Ribbon, but Hubs stuffed me into the car, mumbling something about my "inability to conform."

I have a better idea. We'll hire a rooter bus with a paid, teetotaling driver, load up thirty to forty wine-loving friends, and taste the wine like the good Lord intended. All the way to the toes.

"A woman past 40 should make up her <u>mind</u> to be young; not her face."

~Billie Burke

The Midlife Crisis.
Not Just for Men Anymore

IN THE ONGOING and age-old battle for equality between the sexes, women have recently achieved a new victory. It seems that Science has determined that men aren't the only sex to experience a midlife crisis. Studies show that women are just as likely as their Hubbies to take a little reality detour between the ages of forty and sixty.

This is good news, ladies.

Historically, *he* got to shave his head, start hitting the gym every night, buy a Porsche, and take up weekend hang gliding with a leggy, blonde, twenty-two-year-old instructor named Trixie. *We* suffered quietly (or not) through hot flashes, night sweats, mood swings, and hips spreading faster than hot marshmallows over a campfire.

Before Science leveled the playing field, when a man woke up one morning and decided to upend his entire life with new priorities and pursuits, friends and family simply sighed and told one another, "He's just going through that midlife thing. Be patient. This will pass." Essentially, an adult version of "Boys will be boys."

If we got up one day and chopped our hair off, scheduled an overdue boob lift/tummy tuck combo, and sold all of our clothes to pay for a hunky Sherpa to hike us through the Himalayas, there'd be a swift and strenuous intervention by loved ones trying to bring us back to sanity. But now, science has provided us an excuse.

It's not our fault. It's somehow programmed into our genetic makeup, and we now have the same plausible deniability that our partners have over responsibility for our actions.

But how do we know if we're going through an actual midlife crisis or just bored and needing to change the color scheme in the master bedroom?

➤ **You often fantasize about a simpler life**. Suddenly, you start noticing you have too much crap, too many obligations, too much debt. Just *too much*. You start looking at perennially sunny, laid-back tropical islands as potential homes, not vacation destinations, while quietly off-loading everything in your garage, attic, or storage unit to friends and family. Marriage counselors suggest this can actually be healthy, as long as you're only giving away *your* stuff.

➤ **You're bored with things that you used to enjoy**. Everything feels like "been there, done that." Movies, books, travel, your weekly bowling league, your home, your partner, your sex life. Nothing seems exciting anymore. We're assuming here that you're not much fun right now, either, which, if nothing else, explains your boring sex life.

➤ **You're looking up ex-partners on Facebook**. Reminiscing about old loves, and wistfully remembering the intensity of young love. Never mind that those were the crazy years, when you dumped that loser for sleeping with your sister. And your mom.

> **You read obituaries, looking for old classmates**. And you become slightly irritated when the notice doesn't tell you how or why they died. How can you tell yourself it won't happen to you if you don't know what "it" is? Who cares if the family "wants to keep it private"? Seriously, that's just selfish.

> **You're angry at your spouse for keeping you tied down**. Yes, we all know that you could have been a Grammy-winning country superstar if Hubby hadn't gotten you drunk and knocked you up at nineteen, killing your dreams. Since it would have been difficult for him to achieve this feat by himself, while you were out feeding the homeless, we're assuming you participated at least marginally in the premature demise of your epic stardom.

> **You suddenly desire a new, more passionate relationship**, often with someone much younger. Yeah, this one always ends well. It's the sexual equivalent of cleaning your house by backhoeing your living room. Exciting for a moment, but generally results in massive cleanup and casualties, when it's over.

> **You experience symptoms of bipolar ambition**. Some days, you're a tweaked-out squirrel, manically trying to get 'er *done* before you die, locking yourself in your office after giving emphatic instructions to the family that, unless there's blood or fire, *"Do not come through this door."* Other days, you stay curled up on the couch with bunny slippers and bed hair, watching *Little House* (yes, all ten seasons), because what's the use? You're a big fat loser, and you're never going to accomplish anything, anyway.

➤ **You've developed a new obsession with exercise and nutrition**. You suddenly realize that your sedentary, chemically processed lifestyle over the past fifty years is probably going to catch up with you. By Thursday. So now you're determined to run five miles every morning and cut out gluten, carbs, fats, dairy, salt, and all alcohol, including cough syrup and mouthwash. Congratulations. You've just added a year to your life, but you're now bitchy and have no friends.

➤ **You're on a quest to look young again**. As seen in the faces of many Hollywood stars, the relentless pursuit of youth appears to be a choice between looking fifty and looking freaky. Over-lifted, over-Botoxed, over-tightened, and over-tucked, with foreheads that don't move and boobs that don't bounce, we now look vain and stupid, not young. At fifty, *youth* is no longer at option. Class and style, however, are timeless.

So, what do we do when we hit that midlife Oh-my-God-I'll-never-be-young-again wall?

❖ **Stall on any life-changing decisions**. "Hubby left the toilet seat up for the 10,000th — and *last* — time, and now I'm leaving his selfish ass" will not roll back the years.

❖ **Hang out with girlfriends**, especially the good ones who nourish your soul. If it's happening to you, it's probably happening to some of them. Good girlfriends can keep us sane (and keep our marriages and careers intact) during an insane time.

❖ **Find a cause**. My mother always told us, "If you're having a problem you can't seem to fix, go out and help someone else with theirs." Works every time.

❖ **Be patient**. Your Himalayan Sherpa would say, "This, too, shall pass." It will. And it's so much nicer when you come out the other side and discover that your life, surprisingly, is actually pretty damn good.

"I say really stupid things
sometimes.
When I go back and watch some
of my old interviews
from when I was younger,
I just cringe."

~Michelle Pfeiffer

12 Stupid Things People Love to Say

WE'VE ALL heard them. We might have even said them from time to time. "It's like comparing apples to oranges." "It's for the best." "When God closes a door, He opens a window." We pepper our daily conversations with a lengthy list of clichés and sayings that, regardless of our good intentions, may or may not actually *make sense*.

There are a few popular expressions I hear almost daily that never fail to make me wince. Depending on the amount of wine I've had, I can usually resist the overwhelming temptation to say "Whut??" (although not always; I have been known to spark spontaneous verbal sparring matches with drunk party guests, long-suffering parents, and self-proclaimed-but-idiotic religious experts). On a recent evening rant about expressions that make me crazy, Hubs commented he was surprised I hadn't written an article about them.

So I did.

The Top 12 Stupidest Things People Love to Say:

1. **"There but by the grace of God go I."** Seriously, dude? So, what you're telling me is that God loves *you* and therefore is gracious in His forgiveness of *your* screw-ups, but that poor sot over there must have pissed the Big Guy off, because *his* life sucks. Your God sounds a tad vindictive. Best haul your fortunate butt to church, pronto, and say thanks, before He decides you're a loser and takes his grace elsewhere.

2. **"Do you want an honest answer?"** No. Actually, I prefer that you continue to lie to me every time you open your mouth, as you've obviously been doing, since you suddenly seem compelled to offer honesty as a heretofore unexplored option.

3. **"I don't mean to be critical, but..."** But BOOM, you're going to be. Whenever someone starts a sentence with, "I don't mean to be critical/judgmental/mean/fill-in-the-blank-with-something-negative," that's *exactly* what they're going to be. If you don't mean to be critical, don't be. Otherwise, just spit out your criticism or judgment without preamble. You're not any less of a bitch just because you say you don't mean to be one.

4. **"All things in moderation."** Well, *that's* boring. Where's the passion, the energy, the future blog post?? Moderation may be fine for some things, but moderation doesn't make memories. "Here lies Vikki. Beloved wife and mother. She did all things in moderation. She was the most boring person on the planet." Yeah, no. I'm thinking, "Here lies Vikki. Full Steam Ahead, Damn the Consequences. She was crazy, but damn, she was *fun.*"

5. **"Good things come to those who wait."** Then the world is full of lazy freeloaders who are about to strike it rich, because they've waited for *years*. Good things come to those who go out and make it happen. I would *never* tell my child to wait for what he wants. Worst. Advice. Ever.

6. **"Money is not important."** Almost always pretentiously stated by someone who has a buttload of it. I've never heard a poor person say this. But, if you have a lot and it's not important to *you*, feel free to give me your banking information.

7. **"God never gives you more than you can handle."** So what you're saying is if God determines I'm a strong person, He just might heap all sorts of tragedy upon me, simply because "I can take it"? Wow. I think I'd prefer God thought I was a total wreck, so He'd never give me anything bad and my life would be all unicorns and rainbows all the time. Seriously, people. Y'all need to consider a different church, where God is a little kinder to His flock.

8. **"My bad."** In the *old* days, we used to say, "I'm sorry," which was classier and less flippant. "My bad" is juvenile and patronizing. No one over the age of twenty should use this as an apology for a mistake. Ever.

9. **"It was in the last place I looked."** Well, duh. We're assuming that once you found said lost item, you quit looking, because, well, you found it.

10. **"I could care less."** Let's clear this one up for all time. This means you *could* care less. As in, "I don't care much, but it *is* possible to care less than I do right now." What most people are trying to say is, "I *couldn't* care less," meaning, "It's not possible for me to care less about this." I'm a grammar buff. You can shoot me now.

11. **"That's just the way I am."** Rarely used to excuse one's *better* traits. ("I give $1,000 every year to the Food Bank, because that's just the way I am." Never heard at a bar.) This one is usually reserved to justify behaviors we *should* change but have no current plans to do so, and is often offered up by the same people who believe that all negative behavior is an uncontrollable and incurable disease. If you're happy and you've got lots of friends who love you, rock on with your rebel self. But if no one wants to be around you because, well, you're a total jackass, you might consider being a little less "just the way you are."

12. **"It's only twenty bucks."** Over the years, I've learned that people who use the word "only" before any amount of money usually owe it to you. "What's the big deal? It's only a hundred bucks." "Don't worry. I'll pay you back next week. It's only fifty bucks." "I'm still broke, so you'll have to wait on the money you loaned me. But it's only two hundred bucks. You can afford it." Well, here's my thought on that. If it's "only" two hundred bucks, then how about you give it to me and it can be "only" two hundred bucks out of *your* checking account??

So there you have it. I feel so much better now. I hope I haven't offended you in any way. If I have, my bad.
STOP THAT. I'm sorry. Are we still friends?

"If two of you are giggling in
bed, you're doing it right.
If only one of you is giggling,
not so much."

~ Author Unknown

16 Reasons Women Love Married Sex

I WAS HAVING lunch with a girlfriend who remarried about a year ago, and, anticipating her one-year anniversary, she waxed on throughout the afternoon about how beautiful her wedding was (that's true; it was), how in love they were (also true), and how it was the "happiest day of her life." *What??*

You're kidding, right?

I always struggle when people put superlatives in the past. My knee-jerk response is, "Really? So you've never been as happy as you were on *that* day? It's all been downhill since then?" Hubs and I got married seventeen years ago. I shudder to think that our wedding, however beautiful, means my happiest day is seventeen years behind me.

Later that week, I heard a similar comment from a girlfriend who was talking about her dating sex life, circa 1996. "That was the best sex I've *ever* had," she said with a sigh and a dreamy smile. Wow. Not only was it apparently better than anything she's had since, the gentleman involved is not the man to whom she's currently married. I suggested she keep that little nugget to herself during any future pillow talk with the hubby.

But refusing to believe that, once we get married, our "best sex *ever*" is destined to become a dusty, sporadically dredged-up memory of an old flame, I rounded up my group. We all got together with some wine to debate the issue: is dating sex really better than married sex? Does married sex inevitably become routine and boring, while dating sex is always hot and exciting? Is the "best sex we've ever had," like our wedding day, just *over*?

Bahahahaha.

Married sex *rocks*. Here's why:

1. **Morning sex is easier.** You're already in bed and naked. All you have to do is roll over. By the time your single friend shows up for her morning booty call, Date Guy is out the door and on his way to work.

2. **You're with someone who loves you exactly the way you are.** He's seen your crazy, and you still turn him on. Besides, some men *like* crazy. If Hubs didn't, I'd still be single.

3. **There are no freaky surprises.** If he likes getting busy with it in public places, has weird pet names for his junk, or prefers gymnastics-level positions, by the time you're married, you already know about it.

4. **There's no confusion about the direction of relationship.** "Last time we had sex, he didn't call for two weeks." "He called me Carol. My name is Suzanne. Is he sleeping with somebody else?" 'He took a phone call out of the room. OMG. Is he *married*?"

5. **There's less prepping involved.** When you're single and out on a booty call, you're expected to be washed, waxed, and wearing your "do me" outfit at all times. Married sex is less demanding. Hopping up to do the deed on the dryer doesn't usually require shaving your legs. Or thong underwear.

6. **You can try new things without fear of looking like an idiot or being laughed at when you fall off the bed.**

Admit it. Sex can be funny. Toppling off the bed (or each other), farting, foot cramps, uncomfortable positions or surfaces, the dog scratching to get in, or Jehovah's Witnesses knocking on your door while you're in the middle of getting your skippy on can result in spontaneous hilarity, temporarily derailing your trip to erotic Zen. But, later, you can always pick up where you left off. You'll both still be together at home.

7. **No more 2 a.m. Walks of Shame** past the lobby doorman to your car in your strapless little black dress and bare feet, carrying your stilettos because you can't get them back on. Clean clothes, your blow-dryer, and Peabody, your cat who pees in your shoes if his breakfast is late, are all right there next to you. Sleep well.

8. **Booty calls are simple**. He's in the living room. You're in the kitchen. Walk down the hall and go git it.

9. **No more faking it**. There's no pressure to rush to the finish because Date Guy has got to get home. (He's working early tomorrow, and it's taking you too long, so you need to put a wiggle in it, Missy.) You've got all the time you need to get your happy dance going, without the need to make him feel like he accomplished something he didn't.

10. **It doesn't require visits to the local clinic after every yippee**. Assuming you are both monogamous, no worries about STDs or unknown partners in the mix.

11. **No more condoms**. They're a hassle, they feel weird, and the last time your hot date stood before you wearing nothing but a lime-green, ribbed-latex tube on his penis, you laughed so hard, he left with his clothes in hand, and you've never seen him since.

12. **There's no more worrying that you don't know what he likes and what not-so-much**. And you don't have to learn it all by the second attempt. It takes away the anxiety about "getting it right" and having those humiliating, "I told you this last time, Baby; I like it *that* way" conversations in bed.

13. **No fears of being laughed at or judged when we ask for something specific**. We can just blurt it out, without fear of rejection or ridicule. We can have "big girl sex." We're fifty-plus. We get to ask.

14. **You don't have to drink and drive to your booty call** (or back home after). You're already home. And you've got wine.

15. Unless you're married to Charlie Sheen, you don't have to worry that **your nude photos** will be splattered across Facebook and Twitter, or that **the incredibly bad homemade video** you made one drunken night will be submitted to the upcoming Fox12 reality show, *Menopausal Porn Stars.*

16. **You never have to ask, "Was it good for you?"** By this time, you know what to do and how to tell if you're doing it right. And so does he.

It kills you to see your children grow up.
But I guess it would kill you quicker if they didn't"

~Barbara Kingsolver, *Animal Dreams*

18 Things Your Adult Child Never Wants to Hear

A RECENT Google search for articles on empty nest syndrome turned up almost four million posts. Apparently, it's a universal phenomenon among the boomer generation.

Our kids are leaving home, pursuing further education and careers, getting married, having our grandbabies, buying homes, and generally living life quite happily without our round-the-clock helicopter parenting. We've known from the little guy's first day that this time would come, but we still aren't prepared. *We're not ready.*

We're not ready to miss them so much. We're not ready to "Stop worrying, Mom." We're especially not ready to *stop parenting.*

But parenting an adult with a wife, two children, and a dog is vastly different than parenting a young child. One of the most profound changes comes in the way we communicate with our grown progeny. It's difficult to remember that we are no longer *raising* them. We don't get to pass judgment on their behavior, nor can we criticize their priorities or decisions (unless our aim is to sever all ties, in which case, tell them everything you're thinking). As hard as it is, we must now treat them as *adults.* This often requires some serious tongue-biting, lest we blurt out something too, well…, parental.

1. **"You're doing that wrong."** Especially when he hasn't asked you for help. This is often stated when he's not doing it *your* way. And *never* say this while there are other people in the room. Now you just called him idiot in public.

2. Any sentence that starts with **"If you want my advice…"** If you have to ask, he doesn't.

3. **"I'm disappointed in you."** Often the parenting bat of choice for couples with young children, who'll usually do anything to regain Mom and Dad's approval. An adult child is more likely to reply, "Back atcha."

4. **"Your wife needs to…"** *You* need to Stop. Talking. Never, *ever* criticize your son's wife, in any discussion. He loves her, and now *she* is the most important woman in his life. If you draw a line in the sand, guess who wins.

5. **"When I'm dead, you'll wish you spent more time with me."** Maybe, maybe not. Maybe he's not coming over because you say stupid crap like that.

6. **"You wouldn't be so broke if you didn't buy so much expensive stuff. Do you really *need* a sixty-inch TV?"** Unless you paid for it, it's NOYB, as in "None of Your Business." If he's spending beyond his means, life will find a way to let him know. In the meantime, he won't have to shoot the messenger. Yes, that would be you.

7. **"I can't believe what you kids pay for your phones. When we were little, all we had was a dial-up phone with a party line. And we were *grateful* to have it."** Remember how *you* felt when your mom and dad told you these stories? Yeah, that.

8. **"You've been married for two years. When can we expect the pitter-patter of little feet?"** Sorry, but this is also NOYB. The decision to have a child is limited to the two participants only. If you're good and behave nicely, you'll be notified at the appropriate time.

9. **"Well, you can't be too hard up if you're going to that expensive gym every day."** Unless they're asking you for money, limit all commentary about their finances to, "I'm sure you'll figure something out." All other options will inevitably lead to future whining from you about "why my kids never tell me anything."

10. **"Have you gained weight?"** Just because he came out of your woo-hoo doesn't mean you automatically have the right to forever comment on his appearance. It's no less rude than if he walked into your house and said, "Hi, Mom. Wow, have you put on some weight?"

11. **"You don't call often enough."** Enough for whom?

12. Upon entering his messy house, **"How can you live like this??"** (usually followed by a loud sigh and an uncontrollable urge to start cleaning). It's *not your house*. How someone chooses to live in their own home is NOYB. If you can't stand it, visit with him at your house.

13. **"Well, don't expect *me* to pay for that."** Did he *ask* you to pay for it? Or are you just inferring that any discussion of money means he's got his hand out?

14. **"You need a haircut."** He's thirty, with a wife and two kids. He gets to wear his hair any damn way he pleases. (And if he truly needs a haircut, his wife will make sure he gets one.)

15. **"Are you two saving any money?"** Their marital finances are off limits. (Unless, of course, they're living with you

and saving money to someday move out, in which case you should be getting a weekly cash flow report.) But keep in mind they're probably saving as much as you did at twenty-five. Yeah, pretty much zero. They'll figure it out. Just like you did.

16. **"How's your sex life?"** The only thing worse than being asked to tell you about *his* is you responding with information about *yours*. And whether he's five or fifty, no child ever wants to hear that Mom and Dad are now doing, or have ever done, the freaky.

17. **"Your father is being a jackass. Can I come stay with you two for a while?"** They might say yes, but you've got to know that, when they hang up the phone, they're screaming, "*NOOOOOO!*" Save your relationship with your son and DIL. Work out your marriage in a hotel.

And the universally recognized Mac-Daddy statement, guaranteed to strike terror in young married couples around the globe:

18. **"I saw the house next door was for sale, so I put in an offer!"** 'Nuf said.

"One of the many things nobody ever tells you about middle age is that it's such a nice change from being young."

~ William Feather

My Fairy Godmother Told Me She Could Make Me 20 Again.
I Said No, Thank You

IT'S GENERALLY accepted that Americans live in a youth-oriented society. In our country, beauty is defined by perky boobs, toned arms, and butts like tiny peach pits. We take our kids to college and reminisce about bright, open-ended futures. We envy the *possibilities* of youth as much as we do their smooth, unlined faces. It can seem like the young truly do have it all.

But do they really? Is age twenty to forty the best time of your life, after which every birthday is another day spent sobbing into two pints of Ben & Jerry's Schweddy Balls with a box of wine?

Hell, no.

It's largely true that, during our twenties and thirties, it was possible to look fabulous in sweatpants and Uggs, and the world was pretty much our playground. But there was also a lot of angst and uncertainty.

We spent many of those years searching for "the one." Countless awful dates, multiple crashed-and-burned relationships, and a more than a few broken hearts, until we finally found the person we wanted to spend our life with. (Or at least the next four years, until you left his loser ass because he slept with Little Dexter's pre-school teacher.) Then, the search began again.

After the second (and hopefully final) wedding, we began our new lives faced with mortgages, car payments, and massive student loans from that out-of-state college we just had to attend because our high school love, Biff, was enrolled there. (It didn't matter to the Student Loan department that Biffy dumped us after the first year. They still wanted their money back). We were building careers and juggling schedules. If we had children, there were 2,000 soccer games (1,999 of them in the rain), eighteen-plus themed birthday parties (per kid), band lessons and ballet recitals, adorable toddlers who became uncommunicative teenagers seemingly overnight, *their* college expenses, and health insurance for *everybody,* including the dog.

Those decades were fun, but they were a lot of *work.*

This year, I'm turning sixty. Nope, not fifty (the universally recognized middle-age birthday). 6-0. Sixty is not the "new forty" or even the "new fifty." It's *sixty.* If I keeled over dead after breakfast, my kids would say, "She lived a full life." But would I change it? Not a chance.

Old age brings its own rewards. If you're not here yet, this is what you can look forward to:

- ❖ **Menopause. As in,** *it's over.* No more chronic fatigue. No more night sweats and sleeping on cold, wet sheets because you're too exhausted to get up and change them. Again. No more mood swings that suddenly cause your hubby to remember he has plans to go out with a buddy. Again. *No more hot flashes.* (You might consider circling through town and apologizing to all the waiters you screamed at because "It's *too damn hot in here!*" I'm sending cards.)

❖ **Less worry about how things will turn out**. By sixty, we pretty much know what we're going to accomplish with our careers. We have a good bead on what our kids are going to be like as adults (since they already are). We're either single or married, but either is probably by choice. Most of life's Big Questions have been answered.

❖ **You don't care as much about what others think**. You can be *you*. Sing in your car. With the windows down. Funky dance in the park. Wear makeup every day. Or never. Wear yoga pants to church. Wear your motorcycle jacket with everything. Fly your freak flag whenever and wherever you want. Do you really care what that fifty-year-old Zumba queen next to you is thinking as she watches you bust your goofiest moves? Tell her to lighten up and get out of the way, baby, because you do a mean grapevine.

❖ **You can wear comfortable shoes**. Because we all know that life is better with happy feet.

❖ **You can ditch the minivan** and get the car you actually *want*. A two-seater, bright-red, convertible sports car. Or maybe you think the neighbor's tiny yellow electric car is the coolest thing *ever*. Yep, they're both impractical as hell, but guess what? You're sixty. Drive whatever the hell you want.

❖ **You never have to buy in bulk again**. Cancel your Costco membership and start buying that wildly expensive but oh-so-yummy fresh shrimp from the local Saturday market, because you're no longer buying food for the entire Varsity football team. Added bonus: Your storage capacity will triple when every closet isn't stuffed with jumbotrons of toilet paper and ketchup.

❖ **You get to say No.** "No, I can't come over and help you find your son's lost gerbil. I'm in the middle of *Magic Mike*." "No, I'm not dog-sitting Sir Craps-a-Lot, because that's what he does on my carpet every time he stays here." "No, I can't go out to dinner because I haven't showered all day and I don't plan to." You're not being selfish. You're being honest. We can do that now.

❖ **We've come to terms with our bodies.** In our younger years, we could measure the shifting of our body parts with the accuracy of a California geologist tracking the movements of tectonic plates. Now, we know we can't outrun gravity, and we begin to accept inevitable changes in our bodies. We're more relaxed about what we can fix and what we can't. And we're over it.

❖ **You get to buy fun stuff.** You already have a home, a car, and a savings account. And the kids have moved out (haven't they?). Now you can buy all the cool crap you've always wanted but had to back-burner because you were putting three mini-adults through college. It doesn't have to be *necessary*. It just has to be *you*.

❖ **You get grandkids.** Grandchildren, with that heart-melting clean-baby smell and those adorable faces. They love the bejesus out of you, no matter what, because you're…, well, *Grandma*. You can love them, spoil them, and treat them like the little heirs to throne they are. Then you get to give them back to their original owners and go get a massage. Best. Deal. *Ever.*

"Never let a bad memory get in the way of a good memoir."

~ Joanie Levenson

What Not to Say to a Writer

WRITERS ARE a funny breed. We're highly imaginative and often extroverted but spend vast amounts of time alone. We freely share huge pieces of our lives without reservation or filters, but we're also oddly reserved, preferring to spend our time connecting with people on paper rather than in real life.

We're fiercely private about our writing until it's "ready," then we pray that someone, *anyone*, will want to read it when we're done. We write early in the morning, before our "real job." We write after work, when we're tired and just want to watch a movie and have a glass (or a bottle) of wine. We write on weekends, with spouses and kids knocking on our locked doors, wanting to know if we're coming out or should they just leave our dinner on a tray in the hallway. We write in the shower or waiting at the doctor's office or when we're driving.

There are over 1,000,000 books published in the U.S. every year. On average, they sell less than 250 copies each. Studies repeatedly remind us we have less than a one percent chance of being stocked in the average bookstore.

So, knowing there's a near-zero chance of being "successful" or getting that call from Oprah that will catapult us to instant fame and fortune, what would compel a sane person to keep doing it??

If you're truly a writer, writing is not a choice. Writers *have to write.* Our brains are permanently set to "How can I write about this?" All. The. Time. We view the world in terms of *words.* Words that bounce around in our heads, compelling us to *write it down,* whether on a blog, an email to friends or family, or on the back of a napkin at the local cantina.

Most writers, regardless of their previous success, are inherently insecure about their work. We live in constant fear that the world will suddenly discover we're quasi-talented hacks and our time would better be spent learning to yodel for our future, more appropriate career in goat herding. If you know a writer, we ask that you take pity on our weirdness and try to avoid certain comments or questions in our casual conversations. We'll love you for it and promise not to put you in our next book.

- **"I loved your book. I've loaned it to everyone I know."** I love that you loved it (truly, I do), but I can't pay my bills from the sale of one book.

- **"When are you going to write another one?"** Writing and publishing a book is like Mr. Toad's Wild Ride: it takes a staggering commitment of time, energy, and, often, money, after which we're left lying in an exhausted, broken heap on the side of the road, unsure if we've got it in us to ever do it again. But we'll let you know.

- **"I heard only 1% of new authors are ever successful."** That's true. And thank you for reminding me.

- **"I'm going to wait and buy one when the price goes down."** Swell. I'll let you know when it hits Powell's Online Bargain Basement. I'm sure it won't be long.

✍ **"We've been friends forever. Don't I get a free copy?"** *I* don't even get them for free. And you're a doctor. Is my next pap smear free?

✍ **"My group is having a raffle next week. Would you like to donate some copies?"** Yeah, sure. I just spent the last two years writing the book and several thousand dollars getting it published, but I welcome opportunities to give away free copies.

✍ **"I'd love to write a book. I just don't have time."** Neither did we. Waiting to "have the time" to write a book is like waiting to have the money to raise a child. It won't happen. If you want to write a book, write one.

✍ **"I'd buy a copy, but I don't read."** Despite Kanye's baffling insistence that this is cool, unwillingness to read suggests an inability to do so. You don't need to read *my* book, but please tell me you occasionally read *something*.

✍ **"Has Oprah called you yet?"** This is a not-so-subtle hint that we haven't really "arrived" if Oprah hasn't tapped us for next week's show. An almost impossible standard that can suck the joy out of what we *have* accomplished.

✍ **"I'd love to stay home all day and write."** So would I.

✍ **"You're self-published, aren't you?"** Yes, because I'm a loser who couldn't get a publishing house to do it.

✍ **"Have you written anything I might have read?"** Since I don't know you and don't know what you like to read, how could I possibly know *that*? Oh, you want to know if I've written any best sellers. No, but thank you for asking.

✍ **"Will you read my manuscript?"** You're really asking if I'll critique it or edit it. Those people are called "editors," and they charge a hefty fee. I'm a writer, not an editor.

⌀ **"Can you make a living writing?"** Absolutely. If you live in a yurt and eat berries out of the forest. And if you don't need a car. Or electricity and running water. Otherwise, as they say, don't quit your day job.

⌀ **"I haven't bought your book yet, but I can't wait to read it."** We have no response to this one.

⌀ **"I found a typo."** You read the entire book, and that's what you took away? Awesome.

⌀ **"I thought your book was kinda funny."** That's like saying, "Your wedding was fine." We want to hear, "It's the funniest book I've read, *ever*. It changed my life." Or something like that.

So, if we meet on the street and you're looking for something to say, a simple "Loved your book" will cover almost every contingency. And if you want to make us smile, "Would you sign it for me?" Or you can make our dreams come true with, "I bought one for all my friends," which will result in an immediate happy dance and lifetime access to our secret stash of wine and chocolate.

"I read recipes the same way I read science fiction.
I get to the end and think,
'Well, _that's_ not going to happen.'"

~ Unknown

Learn to Cook, They Said.
It'll be Fun, They Said

WHENEVER A NEW baby comes into a family, the first year or so is all about how "his ears are huge, just like Uncle Elmo's" or "her smile looks just like Aunt Trixie's."

By the second year, we start looking for positive personality traits, hopefully handed down from beloved relatives. He may have Uncle Dumbo's ears, but he also has his off-the-chart IQ and has already moved on from Mommy & Me classes to baby cello lessons, while Aunt Trixie's mini-me has never met a stranger she didn't like, just like Auntie (a wildly popular stripper at the local gentlemen's club).

Sometimes, the personality and talents of our children remain a gene-pool mystery that just simply *is*.

My sister is a fabulous cook. As in valedictorian of her culinary school. I can't cook. At all. Zero kitchen skills. And not in a cute, "Oh my goodness, my freshly grated coconut needs a touch more browning" way. More of a "Would you like your Pop-Tart toasted, or will out-of-the-bag do?" kind of way.

One year, I was instructed to bring my favorite appetizer to a family dinner. I brought a box of Wheat Thins and two flavors of Cheez-in-a-Can. (C'mon, people: one was *bacon* flavored.)

And so began Sissy's ongoing inquiry at every family event, repeatedly asking Mom, "Are you *sure* she's ours?"

Last evening, Hubs announced that it was time to get the cooking question answered, once and for all. What *exactly* was it about cooking that makes stale Lucky Charms more appealing for dinner than the simplest recipe? Okay. Here goes.

➤ **The finished dish *never* looks like the picture in the book.** Your runny, lumpy pie will bear minimal resemblance to its photographed counterpart, with its lightly browned crust and just the right amount of fruit smooshing out of the perfectly symmetrical slices across the top. So, essentially, you're a failure before anybody even grabs a fork.

➤ **I'm a great multi-tasker, if my task list includes things I do well.** Most meals, however, include more than one dish, and one is expected to get them all edible *simultaneously.* My culinary limitations mean you get one dish at a time. When I finish that one, you can eat it while I start the next one. I tried it once, calling it our "Progressive Dinner," hoping the family would think it was unique and fun, but it never took off.

➤ **My taste buds never surpassed my fifth birthday and are easily entertained by peanut butter and banana sandwiches and microwavable jalapeño poppers.** Why take all that time to cook when I can be happily satisfied with a jar of Nutella and a glass of wine?

➤ **The better you are at it, the more often people expect you to do it.** I have friends whose family members expect them to repeat this process *three times a day.* I laughed for two days, until someone told me that wasn't a joke. Oh. My. God.

➢ **Meal planning for just one week involves seven breakfasts, seven lunches, and seven dinners, excluding snacks and desserts**. Are you *kidding* me?? Devoting my days to multiple feedings for people who are capable of programming three remotes to watch the Big Game, but who have somehow lost the ability to scramble their own damn eggs would result in a call to Domino's Pizza delivery (yes, *for breakfast*) as I crawled out the first open window and headed to the local day spa. See you all at six.

➢ **Every recipe requires something you don't have.** The last time Sissy gave me the recipe for her award-winning cookies, it included an eighth teaspoon of something called "cardamom." It's $11 a bottle. WTF?? This is why people buy Oreos.

➢ **And just when you thought that "simple" recipe from *The Joy of Cooking* might work out, you get to the bottom and it says, "When cool, brush lightly with glaze. Glaze recipe is on page 426. Glaze is best if prepared the day before and allowed to sit overnight."** Seriously, you couldn't have *opened* with that??

➢ **You need a degree in Cooking as a Second Language.** How much is a "smidgen?" What the hell is a "pinch?" "Dust lightly?" Chopped, diced, or minced—what's the difference? And "al dente?" Someone once told me to throw a pasta noodle at the wall, and, if it sticks, it's ready. I was having a ball one day, rocking my favorite country song while I tossed noodles across the room, until I had a wall covered in noodles and an empty pan of water on the stove. I considered just throwing a jar of Ragu on the wall and announcing, "Dinner's ready!" but my family never gets my cooking humor.

➢ **You need a staggering variety of cookware, including utensils, pots, pans, serving trays, mixers, blenders,**

glassware, and on and on it goes, all of which could fund an annual week-long trip to a sun-drenched island with tiny umbrellas in their drinks. *Hmmm*. Yeah, I can be packed in ten.

> ➤ **We live in a world of food intolerances that could send a new cook out on a ledge**, sobbing and clutching a bottle of wine, which, if there is a God, has a screw top. One person needs gluten-free, and another is lactose-intolerant. There's a vegan at every gathering and, of course, the inevitable dieting female who only eats salad but apparently thinks wine is an acceptable substitute for her daily eight glasses of water. You know what, people? Here's the menu. If there's anything on it you can't or won't eat, please feel free (seriously, *please*) to bring your own suitable replacement.

When my son (The Boy) and I moved back to Oregon, he was ten and well-versed in Mom's culinary shortcomings. We went to Safeway for our first big shop to stock the cupboards of our new apartment, and I told him The Rules of the cart. Any item thrown in had to be edible from its original container or microwavable. Period. We had a blast tossing in a fairly impressive variety of almost-food products on a weekly basis for the rest of that year, until Hubs and I got married, and he introduced The Boy to something called a "stove."

Now, at twenty-seven, The Boy is extremely well-versed in how to eat without the need for appliances (or most utensils), which, while not necessarily impressing his wife, absolutely dazzles his nine-year-old son.

Bon Appétit.

"I'm tired of all this nonsense about beauty being only skin-deep.
That's deep enough. What do you want—an adorable pancreas?"

~ Jean Kerr

6 Quick Fixes to Look Better Now
(Warning: Not for the Timid)

HUBS AND I recently decided to schedule a date night. We've both been crazy busy lately and were feeling overdue for some romance time. We chose a date, and then he booked the reservation for two at our favorite child-free restaurant. The only thing left to decide was what to wear. Hubs grabbed his one pair of black slacks, a clean shirt, and black loafers, and he was ready to go. Easy-peasy.

Yeah, that wasn't going to work for me.

Digging through the spare closet in my office, where I keep out-of-season or dressy pieces, I pulled out several choices, but nothing seemed right. One final, persistent search uncovered a fabulous little black dress that I'd forgotten I still had. It looked promising, but it occurred to me that maybe I should try it on "just to check."

Tossing my yoga pants, I gently stepped into the dress. Well, crap. Apparently, twelve months can make a huge difference in one's body shape, because the body in that dress *now* didn't look anything like the body that wore that dress last year. I managed to wiggle into it until it reached my hips, at which point it refused to budge another inch. I gave it a bigger wiggle. Nope. Not a millimeter further. I jumped up and down while trying to pull it up. Still stuck. Obviously, it was time for a clothing intervention.

Ransacking my lingerie drawer, I found my "longline" Spanx and spent the next twenty-five minutes struggling to get them on. Finally victorious but now exhausted and sweaty, I was mortified to discover that, while they shrink-wrapped my waist, hips, and thighs into the next size down, they stopped short at my boobs, which had lost the war on gravity sometime in my late forties.

Burrowing through the drawer, I found my push-up bra with side panels and steel underwires, guaranteed to get the girls back up where Nature originally put them. Swaddled in Spanx and Kevlar, but managing to get the dress over my post-menopausal back fat, I looked in the mirror. It had potential, if I could walk normally while wearing a full-body compression sock.

I waddled over to the chair but couldn't sit down without the dress sliding up my thighs and flashing my girdled body parts. They had all the appeal of trampy butt cracks from low-rider jeans. Ten minutes later, I peeled the whole mess off into a pile on the floor and kicked it into the closet. Back into my comfy, forgiving yoga pants, I headed out the door to find a dress that didn't require encasing my body like a beer sausage at Oktoberfest to get it on.

The morning experience got me thinking about the vast variety of products specifically designed to improve our self-esteem and increase our confidence by hiding, correcting, fixing, or even temporarily eliminating our flaws. For virtually every un-perfect body part, there are products that promise to transport recalcitrant, middle-age body parts back in time. With a little research (and boatloads of disposable income), we can find products that push up our bosoms, tighten our buttocks, reduce cellulite in our thighs, hide redness in our cheeks, de-bloat our bellies, de-puff our eyes, lengthen our lashes, plump our lips, smooth our wrinkles, and change our hair color from blah to bombshell in just thirty minutes. Awesome.

I confess, I'm a big fan of many of these products. Being a sucker for anything that promises youthful beauty without have to join a gym or give up Milk Duds and red wine (yes, for lunch... Don't judge), I tend to whip out my Visa on the first promise. Some work beautifully. Some don't work at all. But a few of the bestsellers are bold and might be worth a try.

1. **Spanx**. Designed to firm and smooth *everything* from boobs to ankles. Our mothers called them "girdles." Be warned. They only work if you buy a size that takes you at least twenty minutes to get into and you're not opposed to breaking a sweat before the big event. And pee *before*. If you're dashing to the porta potty at the Country Music Festival during the closing song, you won't be back in time for the encores.

2. **The Wonder Bra**. Shoves the sisters up to *there*, with water inserts to make them realistically bouncy. Works great until you take it off and he realizes your *real* ones resemble the ears on your sister's twelve-year-old basset hound. It's best to remove this one in the dark.

3. **Butt pads**. Very few things leave me speechless. Intentionally attaching something to your ass, specifically designed to make it look *bigger*... Nope, can't speak.

4. **Bosom Max**. Promises to "lift and enhance bust size" with an electromagnetic-pulse massaging bra. Even without the visual of the pulse action that would look like two ferrets humping inside your bra, it'll magically make your boobs bigger and higher, "without surgery"?? The person who buys this probably also bought the Ab Roller and the Shake Weights. I can't drink enough wine to buy this one. I've tried.

5. **"Cleansing" Kits**. Raved about by Hollywood celebrities, these teas and tablets promise to "cleanse toxins, reduce water retention, and flatten the tummy." Our parents called these "laxatives." Save on shipping. They're available at any drugstore.

6. **Lip Augmentation**. Possibly the stupidest trend *ever*. Channeling Daisy Duck is likely to result in friends and family questioning your decision-making processes on virtually every other issue in your life.

And so it seems that confidence is best achieved by putting as much distance as possible between how we *appear* and what we actually *look like*. Having said that, I'm not quite ready to go natural. Maybe Victoria's Secret could come out with a "Bite-Me-I'm-60" bra that replaces wispy lace with industrial strength strapping?

I'll take one in Nude and one in Black, please.

"Trust me. You can dance."

~ Alcohol

Getting Married? 10 Worst First-Dance Songs, Ever

I LOVE weddings. The flowers, the tulle, the gowns, the anticipation and celebration of everlasting love. It's all so romantic and beautiful. But the *planning* of the blessed event can be anything but.

When summer wedding season hits full stride, wedding planners across the country start scrambling through flurries of last-minute details so the Big Day can go forward without a hitch. There are flowers to choose, dresses to select, hotel reservations to be made, table settings, invitations, vows, menus, music, and myriad other decisions that would stress a yogi Zen master.

Many of these decisions can be made with input from friends and family, but the first-dance song falls solely upon the happy couple. The music, the lyrics, and the artist all blend together in a song choice that says "This is *us*" in a way nothing else can. This is not a decision to be made hastily, haphazardly, or, God forbid, when drunk.

There are dozens of beautiful love songs with positive, meaningful messages and lyrics, and it shouldn't be too difficult to find one that reflects you as a couple and also makes sense to your guests. But there are a few that need to forever remain on the No Fly option list. Songs that sound romantic or appropriate because they're slow and sentimental, but the lyrics or the artist are just *wrong*.

As I was jotting down a few What-were-you-thinking? songs that I've personally watched wedding couples cuddle up and sway to, friends and family chimed in with first-dance songs they've also found a bit baffling. Ultimately I created a list of the **Top 10 Songs You Should Not Choose for Your First Dance.**

1. **"Without You"** (Mariah Carey). *"No, I can't forget the feeling on your face as you were leaving... I had you there, and then I let you go. I can't live, if living is without you..."* While, at first glance, this is a fervent declaration of love ("You left me, so now I want to die"), it's a melodramatic *breakup* song. Not a fortuitous start to a lifetime together.

2. **"How Do I Live?"** (Leann Rimes). *"How do I get through one night without you? If I had to live without you, what kind of life would that be? How do I live? How do I breathe? If you ever go, how do I ever, ever survive?"* Notwithstanding the somewhat desperate neediness this song conveys, it's a little *dark* for a wedding. Again, it's a song about *breaking up.* STOP THAT.

3. **"My Heart Will Go On"** (Celine Dion). *"Every night in my dreams, I see you, I feel you. That is how I know you go on."* From *Titanic.* Yeah, the story of two people who have an intense, once-in-a-lifetime love affair, and then he drowns. This song is *depressing* and will have your guests seeing sinking cruise liners and wet dead people.

4. **"I Will Always Love You"** (Whitney or Dolly). *"If I should stay, I would only be in your way. So I'll go, and yet I know I'll think of you each step of the way. Good-bye. Please don't cry. We both know I'm not what you need."* Seriously?? Yes, this is

a romantic song. No, it's not a wedding song. They love each other, but he's better off without her, so she leaves him, breaking both their hearts. Your guests will be sobbing into their champagne flutes. Nice going.

5. **"Sometimes When We Touch"** (Dan Hill). *"You ask me if I love you, and I choke on my reply. I'd rather hurt you honestly than mislead you with a lie... At times I'd like to break you and drive you to your knees... At times I think we're drifters, still searching for a friend. A brother or a sister, but then the passion flares again."* Wow. In three short minutes, we've covered rejection, spousal abuse, and incest. The trifecta of "Doesn't Belong at a Wedding. Ever."

6. **"Endless Love"** (Lionel Richie). *"My love, there's only you in my life, the only thing that's bright. And your eyes, your eyes, your eyes, they tell me how much you care. No one can deny this love I have inside, and I give it all to you, my endless love."* Unless you're fourteen, this is sappy and juvenile. There's a difference between poignant and gaggingly sweet. Save your guests the risk of mass Kool-Aid coma, and pick a song that relates to people out of middle school.

7. **"Always"** (Bon Jovi). *"This Romeo is bleeding, but you can't see his blood... Now the pictures you left behind are just memories of a different life... When he holds you close, I wish I were him, 'cause those words are mine. And I know, when I die, you'll be on my mind."* So he loves her, but she leaves him for someone else. So he says he'll still be pining for her, presumably years later, on his deathbed. This isn't romantic. It's pathetic and sad.

8. **"Careless Whisper"** (George Michael). *"I feel so unsure as I take your hand and lead you to the dance floor, as the music dies. I'm never gonna dance again. Guilty feet have got no rhythm. Time can never mend the careless whisper of a friend. Now that you've gone, was what I did so wrong?"* Starts out with a

sultry saxophone, but then he announces that he cheated on her, a friend squealed on him, she drop-kicked his loser ass to the curb, and he's blown his chance to ever dance with her again. A song about cheating and self-pity. Save this one for the divorce remix.

9. **"Lovin', Touchin', Squeezin'"** (Journey). *"You make me weep and wanna die, just when you said we'd try. When I'm all alone, you're out with someone else. It won't be long till you're alone, when your lover hasn't come home, 'cause he's lovin', touchin', squeezin' another."* Kind of sexy, with a hot title, until you realize it's about a man who cheated on a woman who's now cheating on him with a guy who's going to cheat on her. Your guests will need an adultery scorecard to keep up.

10. **Anything by Chris Brown**. Lyrics unnecessary. Unless you're into celebrating misogynistic wife-beaters with bad taste, and you find multiple trips to the ER and restraining orders acceptable ways of saying "I love you," pass on this artist. While you're gazing adoringly at each other on the dance floor, your guests will be visualizing Rhianna's battered face.

So, assuming you're not inexplicably committed to any of these songs, put them in the No pile and keep searching. It's worth the effort. And may you live long and happily together.

"There's nothing like a good
cheating song
to make me want to run home to
be with my wife."

~ Steven Curtis Chapman

Caught Cheating on Your Wife?
9 Excuses She'll Never Buy

OKAY. SO you were caught cheating on your wife. We could go either way here. I could spend the next several minutes telling you what a narcissistic tool you are and that you have the morals of an alley cat in heat, but I'm pretty sure your wife has already filled you in on your new Facebook bio that she shared with several hundred of your mutual friends, so I'll move on to something more helpful. Because, right now, if you want to stay married to this woman, the next words out of your mouth need to be selected ex-treme-ly carefully. You've lobbed a grenade into the center of your marriage, and the wrong response to her discovery of the actual agenda for all your late-night "business meetings" could result in a marital apocalypse.

Many women have a scorched-earth policy for cheating spouses. There's no acceptable defense. It's over. Pack your crap and get out.

If you're lucky, your wife might be at least willing to listen to what you have to say. But, if your defense is stupid, condescending, or *blames her in any way*, your next task will be sending out Change of Address forms for your new rental. And if Sugar Baby was anybody she *knows* (or, God forbid, her sister), you'll spend the next three days fishing all your worldly goods out of the backyard pool while she arranges to have your soggy belongings shipped to a ghetto apartment across town. Using your credit card.

So, even though I'm with her on her thoughts on how to dispose of your body without getting caught (and she's having them, trust me), I'm going to help save your sorry ass by telling you what not to say, *ever*, when she confronts you for an explanation.

- ❖ **I was drunk**. What are you? Like, nineteen?? This is a childish excuse, cliché at twenty and absurd at fifty. If you get so incapacitated when you drink that you can't slur your way through "No thanks, I'm married," you need to find an AA meeting. Today. And get a sponsor who likes to babysit, because, obviously, you need to be supervised.

- ❖ **It just happened**. Let's break this one down. You're saying that you were standing there, feeding the homeless, and she walked by on her way to the animal shelter to adopt her third rescue dog, when a tornado hit, blowing off all your clothes and causing you to face-plant on top of her, both of you buck naked and helpless? Well, geez, we almost feel sorry for you now. And your city seems to have a lot of tornadoes. Apparently, three a week for almost a year.

- ❖ **We haven't had sex in weeks**. Maybe because one of you is happily topped up and satisfied. And it isn't her. This is called "shifting the blame," and it will backfire on you. *Big* backfire. What she hears is that every time she doesn't put out, you'll just go somewhere else. Be careful. What's good for the goose…

- ❖ **She came on to me**. So what? You didn't want to hurt her feelings, so you slept with her? Using that logic, your wife would have slept with enough men to start a baseball team, because men have been coming on to her since you two got married fifteen years ago. But *she* said No. She's now rethinking that response.

❖ **It was just sex**. Just sex?? Oh, thank God. She thought it was a violation of everything she cherished about your marriage. She thought it meant you're a lying jerk who thought a couple of hours romping in the hay with some tramp from your office wouldn't implode twenty-five years of marriage and that she'd understand it was "just sex." No biggie. She's also guessing that implies you won't mind if she sleeps with Brad, her ex-boyfriend, who was fabulous in the sack, since it'll be "just sex." If she's out late tonight, don't wait up.

❖ **I didn't mean to hurt you**. Since it wasn't intentional, you're basically still a nice guy. And since you didn't *intend* for her to get hurt, there's no reason for her not to forgive you and let it go. Seriously?? So, while you were sexting, planning secret rendezvous, buying gifts and dinners in out-of-town hotels for another woman (paid for out of the marital checking account), and lying to your wife every single day, you figure that's okay because you didn't *intend* to cause her any pain? This one is likely to make her go ballistic on your loser ass because it's so insulting. You didn't forget her birthday here. *You had sex with another woman*. Only one of those is unintentional.

❖ **There's no spark between us anymore**. This is a classic cheater spin that shifts the blame to her. It's often accompanied by a deep sigh and a sorrowful expression. "I tried, but you just don't seem interested in me anymore. I got so *lonely*." What she hears is that, after twelve years of marriage, the giddy glow has worn off. The relationship doesn't feel "new" anymore. And affair sex is not only new, it's *forbidden*. It's exciting and secret. If your wife could reproduce *that*, you wouldn't have strayed. But, if "new and off-limits" is your barometer for great sex, you're not marriage material and she's better off without you. Period.

- ❖ **It was a mistake**. A mistake is 2+2 = 6. Sleeping with another woman and lying about it for the duration of the relationship is not a mistake. It's an affair. Cheating is a *decision*. You *might* be able to sell the "mistake" excuse if it truly was a one-night stand. But, if you slept with this woman more than once, it was a planned activity. You knew exactly what you were doing, and you chose to do it anyway. She's more likely to forgive you if you don't try to minimize her justifiable anger by calling your extracurricular activities a "boo-boo."

And the #1 "If she snuffs you in your sleep, no jury would convict her" worst possible thing you could say:

- ❖ **It didn't mean anything**. Oh. My. God. Essentially, you've just told her that you risked everything—her happiness, your marriage, your *life* together—for someone who doesn't mean anything to you. Are you *kidding*?? It would be kinder (and more forgivable) if you told her that you fell out of bed, hit your head, and thought the other woman was your soul mate, but that you were clearly delusional because the other woman could never be her, and it will never, ever, *ever* happen again. Then stop talking. She'll let you know what's going to happen next. She's earned the right.

And, next time, keep it in your pants until you get home, m'kay?

"*I always put clothes and family photos
under the mattress,
in case the house burns down.*"

~ Kim Kardashian

What I Learned After 30 Years in the Beauty Industry

I LOVE beauty products. I love the whole beauty industry (except the part where women over forty are unfavorably compared to twenty-year-old swizzle sticks). Over the years, I've learned a lot through it, written a lot about it, and bought a lot of it.

Turning sixty got me thinking about beauty lessons I've learned over the years that remain timeless. We may be thirty-five or seventy-five. We may shop at Nordstrom or Rite Aid. But some things are true no matter what your age.

> **Be careful with cosmetic intervention**. Your face should not look twenty years younger than the rest of you. Too much, and you don't look younger. You look like Kenny Rogers.

> **Wear sunscreen. Every single day**. Only infants can look like Yoda and still be considered cute.

> **Don't make hairstyle decisions after 9 p.m. or more than two glasses of wine.** Spontaneous hair chops while in exhausted or half-gassed conditions (or, God forbid, both)

have resulted in far too many morning-after cries, "OMG, *what was I thinking*?!?"

➤ **No matter what the spa brochure says about their "Painless Bikini Wax," it isn't.**

➤ **Skin care is a forehead-to-boobs concept.** Unless you spend 365 days a year in turtlenecks, the skin on your neck and upper chest gets the same amount of sun exposure as your face and can look just as weathered. If you do it for your face, do it for your boobs. You'll thank me later.

➤ **Every woman should wear red lipstick, even if it's just once in her lifetime.** Something about red lipstick is *powerful*. It's the ultimate "Don't mess with me—you *won't* win" bad-ass makeup product.

➤ **Determine your best asset and buy only those clothes that show it off.** Voluptuous curves, great legs, tiny ankles, pretty arms, beautiful back, great clavicles, long neck? Every woman has *something* that the rest of us would love to have. Dump everything that could double as an emergency pup tent or that makes you feel fat, old, or invisible. Start buying clothes that accentuate your unique fabulousness. It's the best confidence builder *ever*.

➤ **Clean out your closet once a year.** Get rid of the anything that's falling apart, out-of-date, or just plain ugly. Start with the embroidered Christmas sweater (with the eight light-up reindeer) that your ex-husband bought you six years ago (which might explain the "ex" thing). Toss anything, including scarves and shoes, that no longer fits or is uncomfortable *for any reason*. Be ruthless. Then see #7.

➤ **If you do only one thing this year, try a new hair cut or color.** Virtually every reality TV makeover starts with the hair. There's a reason for that. Mall cuts or mousy, faded hair color makes you look like Great-Aunt Agnes from Des

Moines. A good cut or a rich, vibrant color can make your skin glow and your eyes sparkle. Boom.

➢ **Use the best moisturizer you can afford, but recognize that it's topical and has limitations**. If you really want to reduce those crow's feet around your eyes or the vertical creases around your mouth and nose, you're talking injectables (yep, Botox). Start saving up.

➢ **A good magnifying mirror can be your best friend**. How else can we spot those persistent chin hairs every morning or keep that lip pencil actually on the lips?

➢ **Always test a self-tanner before you apply it from head to toe**. Most of them smell nasty and make you look like a bottle of Tang.

➢ **Minimize shimmery products on any part of you that is lined or droopy**. Sparkle catches the eye, making it what people notice first. If your nipples point south like divining rods searching for water and you sprinkle your chest with sparkle powder before your high school reunion, you've just shared that with of the entire class of 1974. And if your eyes are lined or crepey, shimmer can settle in the folds, turning your makeup into a glitter craft project at your grandkid's preschool.

➢ **Never shop when you're depressed**. And never, *ever* shop for jeans or swimsuits when you don't have your game on. If you must buy something when you're feeling blue, shoes are the perfect choice. A new pair of fabulous black boots is guaranteed to pick up your spirits, with no dieting or spinning classes required. Winning.

➢ **Have a professional makeover at least once every ten years**. If you've been wearing the same haircut and the same makeup for ten years, you're in a rut, and you probably look dated. Your skin changes. Products change. Trends change. So should you.

➤ **If you're feeling in a fashion rut (yoga pants and T-shirts, anybody?), enlist the help of your best-dressed girlfriend.** Hit the mall and let her pick out your options. (Alone, you'd just head for the yoga pants department, and you already own eight pairs.) Promise to try on *everything* she hands you. You might be surprised at what you can rock.

➤ **Learn to use hair products. Together.** Mousse *and* volumizing spray, with styling brushes, are often required as hair thins after menopause. Repeat after me, "Product is my friend."

➤ **Makeup product junkies (like me), yes, you can have too many.** Pull out your stash. *All* of it. If you have fifteen lipsticks, five mascaras, a dozen eyeshadows, four concealers, two bronzers, three different self-tanners, and a half-dozen nail polishes, it's time to declutter. Pare down to what you actually wear, and then give the extras to your DIL. She'll trade you for the grandbaby next weekend.

➤ **You can't live a stressful life, with too much alcohol, too little exercise, the not-so-occasional cigarette, a daily dietary habit of pretzels and Diet Coke, *and* have good skin.** Beauty products assume you're a team player. So, take care of the rest of you, and your skin will reflect the love.

"It is important for our friends to believe that we are unreservedly frank with them, and important to the friendship that we are not."

~ Mignon McLaughlin

Best Friends & the Secrets We Keep From Each Other

BEST FRIEND. Bestie. BFF.

No matter what you call her, she's the one person you know will always be there for you. No matter what. When your heart is broken, she's there with a box of tissues, chocolate, wine, and a Taser, in case the guy ever shows his jerk face again and needs to be taken *down*. When you have something to celebrate, she's there with balloons, chocolate, wine, and… well… more wine. She's your "person."

Best-friend status can develop slowly over the years or in an instant. Its hallmark is "We know *everything* about each other," or "We have no secrets," or, my favorite, "We're always *totally* honest with each other."

Really? *Always*??

A recent survey among women ages thirty-five to sixty concluded that women aren't always completely truthful with their BFFs. It seems there are certain things we can't confess, even to her (or sometimes *specifically* to her). Maybe we know the truth would upset her, hurt her feelings, or even damage her marriage. Or maybe it's a secret about *us* and we're too embarrassed to admit it, even to our bestie. So we omit, qualify, spin, and, every now and then, outright lie in our efforts to preserve the friendship and the way we see each other.

Curious as to the validity of these findings, I conducted my own informal research and asked a group of women about secrets they might be keeping from their best friends. I loved the responses.

❖ *"I weigh more than I tell her I do. She knows I'm overweight, but I'm embarrassed to tell her exactly how much. It's weird, because I can tell her how many men I've slept with, but not what I weigh."* This one actually made sense to me. But, then, I refuse to get weighed at my doctor's office because I don't want her office staff to know. Like they care.

❖ *"I exaggerate my husband's income. Her hubby earns almost twice what mine does. I don't want her to think I married a loser."* Personally, I like rich friends. They come in handy when your credit card gets declined after you've offered to buy the next round.

❖ *"I think her husband is a total tool. And so does everybody else in our group. He hits on every woman who can't outrun him. Including me, her best friend. What's wrong with this guy??"* The Mac Daddy of things I'd never tell a girlfriend, no matter how close we were. No woman ever wants to hear that her husband is a cheating jerk and that she's the only one in her book club who doesn't know it.

❖ *"Yes, those jeans give her serious muffin top. Low-rise skinnys should never be a part of the post-menopausal woman's closet. But, hey, if she loves them, I love them, right?"* This one could go either way. Almost every woman, at some point in her life, loves a style or a trend that's less than flattering. So, yes, if she loves it, we love it. But if it's the low-rise, muffin top, butt-crack trifecta of "Give those jeans away. *Now!*" I might blurt it out in a wine-induced moment of total honesty. The world just doesn't need to see another up-close-and-extremely-personal view of a fifty-five-year-old butt crack in a hot pink thong. Some things can't be unseen.

❖ *"She intimidates the hell out of me. With her trendy clothes, gorgeous hair, and perfect skin, every single day. I feel like 'Sara, Plain and Tall' next to her. I'd really love to see her out in yoga pants and no makeup. Just once. But she'd probably rock that look, too. It's just not fair."* I've got one of those. She's gorgeous even in the morning. Slips on her skinny jeans, grabs a T-shirt, and she looks fabulous. I wake up looking like I've been snoring on a plane for five hours. Bed hair, yesterday's makeup, and drool on the side of my face. She says she loves morning sex. Do people actually *have* morning sex?

❖ *"Her adult children still use her like a human ATM. Seriously, they can't pay for anything themselves. Those kids have been 'trying' for years to grow up and don't seem to have made any progress. She's not helping them. She's enabling them."* Be very careful with this one. It's a landmine. Any hint to a mother that her grown progeny is not living like an adult—and that *it's her fault*—can implode your friendship faster than a Hollywood marriage can hit the rocks.

❖ *"Hubby and I haven't had sex in six months, but I'd never tell her that. Based on her tales of nightly, sweaty Kama Sutra sessions, I'm quite sure she's never had a dry spell in her twenty years of marriage. Or probably ever."* I've always wondered about couples who feel the need to tell the rest of us that they do the deed almost every night. And they're both skidding into their fifties. *C'mon,* people. Stop making the rest of us feel like sexual plankton, and admit you're making that up.

❖ *"No, I don't think her grandchildren are the cutest, smartest, and best-behaved toddlers ever born. The little one is two and still looks like Yoda. And the older boy has got a real future in the fast food industry, if you know what I mean."* Ouch. Insult a mother's child, and she's going to be seriously pissed. (Forgiveness may require a really *good* bottle of wine.) But insult a woman's *grandchildren*? Run. Because she will take you *down*.

❖ *"No, I don't agree that she should wear her daughter's clothes because they wear the same size. I'm aware that they're both a size 6. She brings it up during every shopping trip. (Yeah, THAT doesn't make me feel fat in my size-12 granny panties.) But cropped tops with a short denim skirt at fifty-eight? Really??"* Although I agree with the current trend that, after fifty, women should be able to wear whatever the hell makes them happy, there are certain outfits that make specific statements. A cropped T-shirt that says *Don't Touch My Rack* with a blinged-out denim miniskirt on any woman over forty (okay, over thirty) screams, "In case you were wondering, yes, I'm a tramp."

❖ *"I haven't always been thrilled for her when she lost thirty pounds, got that promotion and the big, fat raise, or bought that gorgeous new home with her Ken-Doll husband. I'm still chubby, still in the same mid-level job, and still living in a double-wide next to my parents."* Actually, I heard this one more than once. We want to be happy for you. Really, we do. But, sometimes, we're just a teensy bit jealous. We'll never tell you that, though, because, even when we hate you, we love you.

And so it would seem we are all simply human and the best friendships are about honesty, tempered with generous doses of kindness. And knowing when to shut up and pour the wine.

"My wife says, 'Camping's a tradition in my family.' It was a tradition in everyone's family until we invented the house."

~ Jeff Gaffigan

I Went Camping.
And I Liked It

MY FAMILY, and friends who have known me for more than, say, twenty minutes, know that I don't camp. Hubs has been trying for years to get me fired up about it. "It's *great*," he repeatedly assures me. "The stars are brilliant. The air is clean. It's quiet and peaceful. It's *nature*."

That may be true, but that's not necessarily a selling point for me. While serene, natural settings admittedly hold a modicum of appeal, there are a few sticky spots I struggle with.

- ⌀ **Sleeping in the dirt. On rocks**. Call me spoiled, but I *like* sleeping on soft, comfy mattresses, without having to navigate my REM position around a rocky terrain. Yes, early man used to sleep on dirt and rocks, but then he invented the house. Camping is a step *backwards* in the evolutionary process.

- ⌀ **When nature calls in the woods**. "Pick a tree" is not how I normally choose a place to take care of my private business. I'm *totally* potty shy. Hubs has never seen me pee. *Not once* in fifteen years. He thinks of me as some kind of pee-retaining dromedary, able to travel for weeks at a time without the need for a truck-stop pullover. And for the potty shy, there's no greater nightmare than being spotted by a spouse, a forest ranger, or an entire Brownie Scout troop, squatting with my naked woo-hoo visible from every point on the compass, undoubtedly directly over a patch of poison oak, because I have no freakin' clue what it looks like, causing me to spend the rest of the week with my hand down my pants, scratching my lady parts like a twerking hillbilly.

⌀ **Packing lists that require a disturbing variety of bug repellants**. Sprays, lotions, clip-ons, candles. You need them all. Voluntarily spending the weekend in a place that advises five or more products to keep from being eaten alive by insects is somewhat reminiscent of swimming at a beach that hosts a shark watch tower. If that water requires a shark watcher, I'm not getting in it.

⌀ **Bathing in ice-cold streams**. Showers are like my mini-spa. Hot, leisurely, with lots of suds. I get some of my best writing inspiration in the shower. It's also a great place to have imaginary arguments with Hubs (which, obviously, I always win), thus negating the need to have them in real life. Splashing in a freezing creek, possibly with a stranger from the next tent over, my teeth chattering and goosebumps on high alert, is not conducive to creative thinking or marital problem solving. My brain is too busy screaming, *Why am I here??*

⌀ **Bears**. They're big, ferocious, and usually hungry. Where we see a tent with four people in sleeping bags, they see a canvas microwave filled with Hot Pockets.

Poor Hubs has not been able to overcome my arguments, despite his enthusiastic descriptions of romantic twilight evenings, lit only by stars and insect-repelling candles.

Then, one day, his parents (veteran trailer campers) suggested we try a trailer as a fun compromise. Hubs gets his wilderness experience, while I get a real bed, an indoor potty, *and* a hot shower. Who knew?

A few days later, they pulled up with a 27-foot trailer in tow. "It's yours," they announced proudly. "Try it out for the summer. If you like it, keep it. If you don't, we'll just sell it back." It was an offer we couldn't refuse.

Immediate exploration uncovered a microwave, queen-sized bed, indoor toilet/shower, hot water, fridge, and enough storage space for a week's worth of clothes *and* red wine. This could work.

After brief instructions on towing requirements, site hook-ups, and something about dumping various colors of water at the trip's end, we were set to go. The next weekend, we packed up and headed to a popular woodsy campground with another couple (separate trailers, of course). Trailer salespeople love to wax on about how a small trailer can logistically sleep six people. I don't know six people well enough for that kind of sleeping arrangement. A friend of Hubs's commented, "A trailer drinks six, feeds four, and sleeps two." Nailed it.

By the second day, I was hooked. It was *wonderful*. We slept. We ate. We drank. We talked about everything and nothing. I read three books. (We both agreed: no laptops, tablets, or cell phones allowed.) We were unplugged, and I loved it.

On the last night, as the temperature dropped, we built a crackling campfire, and the four of us sat in a small circle, bundled up and toasty, sharing wine and swapping hilarious stories about misspent youth. As the evening went by, someone suggested we make s'mores.

"What the hell are *s'mores*?" Hubs asked.

Conversation stopped faster than if he'd announced, "By the way, I've decided to shave my junk."

Even *I* knew what s'mores were. "How can you not *know* this??" we all asked. "They're a staple at every kids' camp. You've never had a s'more?"

"Nope," he replied.

"You'll love them," we assured him. "They're *fun*."

Lining up the Hershey bars, marshmallows, and graham crackers, I proceeded to show Hubs how to layer them into a gooey delight by toasting the marshmallow and using it to melt the chocolate. He stuck his marshmallow-topped stick into the fire, preparing for his first, long-overdue s'more experience.

A couple minutes later, Hubs pulled his marshmallow out and found a charred, still-flaming ball. Seeing his dubious expression, the three of us burst out laughing, yelling, "Blow it out! Blow it out!" He tried several big puffs, but only succeeded at exploding it into a dozen blackened, sticky pieces that somehow back-blew into his beard and down the front of his sweatshirt, one flaming chunk landing on the back of his jeans.

By now, poor Hubs was running around the campsite, yelling, "Hot, hot, hot!!" and repeatedly smacking himself in the face, trying to get the hot, gooey marshmallow out of his beard. We were all doubled over in laughter, pointing and yelling that his pants were on fire.

"Hot, hot, hot!"

"Your pants are on fire!"

"Hot, hot, hot!"

"Your pants are on fire!"

"Hot, hot, hot!"

"YOUR PANTS ARE ON FIRE!"

"Holy shit! My pants are on fire!"

I know, we're all going to hell, but I haven't laughed that hard in weeks.

As we got him all put out and calmed down, we discovered charred, gooey marshmallow remnants on his clothes, in his hair, on the sand chairs, and even on the blankets, which we spent the next hour or so scraping up.

"Yeah," he grumbled, "s'mores are just super *fun*."

Okay, s'mores are off the list.

But this camping thing? We've reserved spots seventy-five and seventy-six for next weekend.

I can't wait.

"I gave my father $100 and said,
'Buy yourself something that will make your life easier.'
So he went out and bought a present for my mother."

~ Rita Rudner

22 Best Dadisms About Life

THERE ARE MANY different ways to raise children. And when parents differ as to which one of those ways is the "best," debates on the topic can become emotionally heated. Whether your style is more Pa and Ma from *Little House* ("We just hug it out"), the Jolie-Pitts ("Discipline stifles a child's creativity"), or the Duggars ("My child does. not. lie."), the one thing we can all agree on is that *parenting is hard*.

Most of us were raised by busy parents, often in multiple-child households. Our parents started out as avid Dr. Spock fans (not the one from *Star Trek*; the one who wrote the parenting bible for babies in the '60s and '70s). However, they quickly discovered that long, philosophical debates between them and their offspring every time little Billy broke the baby's toys or Baby Buffy bit the dog simply wasn't going to work. They only had eighteen years to take their adorable wee ones from first discovering they had something called "toes" to being socially acceptable, contributing adults ready to be launched into a generally unforgiving society. Mom and Dad were on the clock.

So, parents across the country developed a system of "parenting shorthand." Brief, pithy admonitions and lessons they could chant like mantras until, eventually, each child had assimilated an arsenal of wisdom to take out into the world and live the dream. Some of this advice came from Mom (See "23 Things Ann Landers Could Have Learned From my Mother," in *Who Left the Cork Out of My Lunch?*), and some came from Dad. Today it's Dad's turn.

1. **"Go ask your Mother."** Translated: "This is a terrible idea. You're fourteen, for God's sake. But I don't want to fight with you about it, because I like being the cool parent. So, ask *her* if you can do it, and *she* can 'ruin your life.'"

2. **"Everyone comes from a dysfunctional family. If some families seem normal, have dinner with them at Christmas."** Thank God. I thought it was just us.

3. **"If you don't want to be married to a poor man, don't date one."** Surprisingly practical advice, when you think about it. Also applicable to alcoholics, drug users, and wife beaters.

4. **"Men love it when women come out of the bathroom all smooth, shaved, and smelling good. But we don't necessarily need a visual on how you got there."** To this day, I *always* close the door.

5. **"Men are like buses. Wait on the corner, and another one will come along."** Despite the not-so-subtle implication that I had a strong future in street-walking, this got me through a few college breakups.

6. **"Do what you love, and don't worry about the competition. There's always room, if you're good."** This prevented me from hurling my laptop out the second-story window and into the neighbor's pool on more than one occasion.

7. **"Pay attention to how a man treats his mother. That's how he'll treat you."** It took me three husbands to get this. It's true. Every. Single. Time.

8. "You can do anything a man can do. Drive a stick shift, snake your bathroom drain, or fix a flat tire." Yay me. But what if I don't *want* to?

9. "Other people will judge you by the way you look. Remember that when you're considering a tongue-piercing while looking for a job." Alas, it's true. Go shopping when you look stylish and fabulous, and then go when you're all bed-head, no makeup, and pajama pants. The difference in the customer service you receive is staggering. See #10.

10. "Life's not fair. Deal with it," in response to any wailing on our parts of "That's *not fair*." Dad raised extremely resilient kids.

11. "Be home by 11. Nothing good ever happens after 11:00." Ha. I was nineteen when I discovered that this one was a *big fat lie*. From ages eighteen to thirty, all the good shit happens between midnight and 2 a.m. (But, after thirty, you should know better. After forty, you're too tired. And after fifty, you simply don't care anymore.)

12. "The only way to have more money is to earn more or spend less." The only part he left out was that *earning more* is a hell of a lot easier than *spending less*. Are those boots on sale??

13. "If you need someone else to make you happy, you'll both end up miserable." This might explain my two divorces. Apparently, I'm a bit slow to catch on.

14. "Everything in moderation. Except love. Love with everything you've got. But don't be a stalker." One of my faves. Kind of says it all.

15. "Never do something you don't want to do, to try and get a man to love you. If he doesn't already, this won't get

him there. If he already does, he wouldn't be asking." An effective bit of advice to guard against teenage sex, drugs, and driving the getaway car.

16. **"Even though we agree that I don't know 'everything about everything,' mentioning that during our escalating parent-child discussion will not end well for you."** Yep, we understood what "pouring gas on the fire" meant before we were out of grade school.

17. **"Yes, you can be angry at someone and still love them."** Difficult to absorb as a child, but by fifty-plus, it describes our marriages.

18. **"Always say Please and Thank you. That way, you get more."** A little narcissistic, but still true.

19. **"The first rule of negotiation: What's in it for the other guy?"** Translated, "No one gives a crap what *you* want. They're interested in how you can give them what *they* want." If everybody in the customer service industry got this one, world peace would be achieved.

20. **"If you loan money to a friend, you'll lose them both."** Unfortunately, this is a lesson we all have to learn by experience. I'm still out several hundred dollars from a friend I haven't seen since I loaned her the money. I'm not sure which I want back more.

21. **"Poor planning on your part does not constitute an emergency on everybody else's."** I *love* this. The quintessential "The world does not revolve around you" life lesson.

22. And my all-time favorite: **"Learn to laugh at yourself. You'll never run out of material."** Done.

"As a teenager, you are at the
last stage in your life
when you will be happy to hear
that the phone is for you."

~ Fran Lebowitz

How to Use Your Cell Phone
Without Pissing People Off

A RADIO report the other day stated that two-thirds of all Americans own a smartphone. And this group was non-discriminatory, including doctors, lawyers, SAHM, young children, teens, Boomers, rich, poor, and the homeless. Apparently, we take our cellular communication very seriously in this country.

While I don't have a problem with the fact that cell phone communication, verbal or texting, has become the primary method of connecting (okay, that's a lie; it makes me crazy), I can't understand why cell phone users often behave like bad drivers. Obviously, many drivers apparently think they're the only one on the road, so they can do whatever they damn well please and you can just get out of the way. It appears that many cell-phone addicts think they're the only person talking on one. Or is it that having a cell phone is some sort of entitlement that includes being a total tool every time your personalized ringtone goes off?

It's human nature to occasionally forget we're not the only human on the planet. We pass the time in crowded dental waiting rooms by dialing up the hubby at Safeway and loudly listing the ingredients for Mom's famous fruitcake recipe. We wait for our food in the restaurant by answering every call and shouting out our itinerary to every family member and your boss. We get back to the fight we started this morning with our spouse, sharing our shouted accusations with everyone at the gym. A gentle reminder or "look" from the person next to us may cause us to take it outside, but is more likely to result in a rude finger gesture and a clearly mouthed, "Bite me."

But for those of you who regularly become "that guy" (and you know who you are), frequently becoming the topic of annoyed conversation for an entire restaurant staff and patrons, it's good to remember that this does not make you look important. It makes you look like an arrogant jackass. To avoid this unfortunate distinction, here are some guidelines that you might consider reviewing periodically, so we all continue to love each other and behave nicely.

- ❖ **There will be times when you need to turn your phone off**. Lunch with Mom, attending a wedding (ditto a funeral), a romantic date, church, your kid's piano recital. And (why do I need to say this?) during sex. Movies and TV shows regularly script a couple making steamy whoopee when his cell phone rings. He groans and she rolls her eyes, but they breathlessly *stop what they're doing*. He answers his phone, while she takes the opportunity to check her messages. *Seriously*?? All I can conclude is that you two are doing it wrong.

- ❖ **You don't need to shout anymore**. It's true that, when cell phones first came out, it quickly became the "Can you hear me now?" era, where every call had us running around the house, waving our phones in the air, anxiously searching for the strongest signal, and shouting into the phone, trying to be heard at the other end. That time has passed, people. *They can hear you now*. You can use your inside voice and speak normally. Truly, we don't care about your vacation plans, your horrible boss, or that hot new chick you banged last night at your class reunion.

* **If you text while driving, you should lose your license. Forever**. And while we're at it, we're also taking away your damn phone. If you're that stupid, you shouldn't have either one. I'm not prepared to die because you couldn't remember if your wife picked up your dry cleaning. If you must text while in motion, do it while you're walking. At least we get some entertainment value out of watching you smack face-first into a light post you didn't see because you had your head down, texting a tee time to your golf buddies.

* **"I've got to take this" is not, in fact, always true**. And, in the middle of your five-year-old daughter's ballet recital, you look like a self-important douche. I know this is a tough one, but the world will not come to an end because you're unavailable for a couple of hours while you celebrate your parents' fiftieth anniversary, visit with your ninety-year-old grandmother, or spend a romantic evening with your wife (assuming she hasn't left your inconsiderate ass after fifteen years of hearing "I've gotta take this" in the middle of every date night).

* **If you simply must take a call, take it outside**. As fascinating as your recent colonoscopy undoubtedly was, we all don't need to hear every detail for the entire duration of our meal. And that real estate deal you're trying to close before that jerk at your office beats you out of the commission is really not anything we give a crap about, so get off the treadmill and out of the gym. Or, better yet, go home and take care of your business, then come back and join us.

* **Lower your ring volume**. Since you have your phone permanently attached to your body at all times, or, God

forbid, you insist on wearing one of those ridiculous ear pieces all day long, you don't need the ringer on High. (Honestly, how do you take a shower? Never mind; I don't want to know...) Pick a non-offensive ringtone, then lower the volume a couple of notches. Yes, we can all still hear you and know how important you are. You just won't be quite as *annoying*.

❖ **Don't overshare.** I hear people all the time freely offering up details of their private lives and the private lives of others on their cell phones. While in public. To avoid an ugly scene when your best friend finds out you told a fishing buddy about his mistress during a cell phone call you had while sitting in a restaurant behind his wife's BFF (true story), here's a general rule: If you wouldn't *do* it in public, don't *talk* about it in public.

❖ **Consider the setting.** Nothing kills a Zen retreat or a quiet day of reading by the lake like the persistent ringing of some idiot's cell phone. We get it. You need to be connected to the world 24/7. You're The Guy. Holidays, weekends getaways, and moments of solitude and quiet contemplation are for losers. We understand. And we respect your choices. We'd just like to respect you from a distance.

So there you have it. We're all friends again. Now let's talk about texting.

"Suppose you were an idiot and suppose you were a member of Congress...
But I repeat myself"

~ Mark Twain

Having Sex in Your Car?
The State of Michigan Salutes You

Human nature never ceases to entertain me. We are one crazy-ass creation that, I'm reasonably certain, is not *exactly* what the Big Guy intended.

My favorite morning news highlights are the reports about some idiot who got pulled over the previous night for a possible DUI. This guy skidded over to the side of the road, jumped out, and ran into the bushes, *leaving his wife, infant son, and mother in the car* to hand over to the police his registration (yep, with his address), right before Wifey drove to her attorney's office to divorce Mr. Every-Man-for-Himself, while his mother was trying to figure out what she did wrong during the pregnancy that caused her to produce possibly the stupidest child on the planet.

I can't explain it, but these kinds of stories just crack me up. What was Stupid Guy *thinking*??

A friend recently sent me a link to laws on the books around the country that had me laughing out loud as I tried to visualize what the hell the regulating states had in mind when they were voting. I had to highlight some of my favorites.

Someday, when our children tell *their* children about rallying to support gay marriage and marijuana legalization, *our* generation's legacy is going to be petitioning to repeal a law (see "Alaska," below) that prevents us from knocking back a cold one at the Beer Belly's Saloon & Day Spa with our favorite moose. Go, Grandma and Grandpa.

(Personally, I think, if a fifty-year-old consenting person and an adult moose want to share a pitcher of margaritas and sing bad country songs together, it's between the two of them, and as long as the human promises not to let the moose drink and drive, people should mind their own damn business.)

And since I've always believed that, some days, it's good for the soul to get a little silly, I'm sharing a few.

❖ **Maryland**: *No person who is a tramp or a vagrant shall loiter in any park at any time.* "Tramp" wasn't specifically defined, so we're a little fuzzy on whether they're referring to a slutty/vagrant split personality, a slut *or* a vagrant *or* simply a homeless man who slept with Mrs. Bagbottom, the senator's wife, making them the poster kids for what a vagrant and a tramp look like. Senator Bagbottom ("Baggy" to his constituents) was reportedly partially vindicated by his legal ability to force the canoodling couple to take it across the border to Delaware.

❖ **California**: *You are not permitted to wear cowboy boots unless you own at least two cows.* So that rockin' pair of Frye cowboy boots you bought at Nordstorm last week? You're going to need a photo of a couple of cows, in case you get pulled over.

❖ **Rhode Island**: *Any marriage where either party is an idiot is null and void.* The local courthouse must be a proverbial beehive of activity, as pissed-off spouses storm the gates after every marital spat—("She paid $150 for that haircut! $150! For *that*." "Yeah, but *he* thinks that nineteen-year-old waitress at Mack's 18-Wheel Truck Stop & Diner is hot for his sixty-year-old body. Bahahahaha!")—eager to prove beyond question that their "other half" is, in fact, an idiot.

❖ **Ohio**: *It's illegal to get a fish drunk.* I'm a bit confused as to how you'd get the little vertebrate up onto a bar stool for Jell-O shots. But if you want to party with a fish, go for it. Just remember, staunch denial of his drunken state is your best defense. It's not like they can ask him to say the alphabet backwards.

❖ **Missouri**: *Clotheslines are banned, but clothes may be draped over a fence.* Which explains how my neighbor came to borrow my underwear. Yeah, you can keep those.

❖ **Idaho**: *If a police officer approaches a vehicle and suspects the naked occupants of gettin' busy inside, he must either honk or flash his lights, then* wait three minutes *before approaching the car* (presumably to let the tangled couple find their clothes or at least throw a blanket over their you-knows). If you haven't had sex in a while, this might be sufficient time to git 'er done, get dressed, and share a cigarette. Idaho has one classy police department.

❖ **Kansas**: *If two trains meet on the same track, neither shall proceed until the other has passed.* Uh… Nope. I got nothing. Rumor has it there are still two trains in a standoff that have been parked since 1865.

❖ **Alaska**: *It's considered an offense to feed alcohol to a moose.* What *is* it with states and their need to keep their wildlife sober?

❖ **Alabama**: *Men who deflower virgins, regardless of age or marital status, may face up to five years in jail.* This one was written by men who still used the word "deflower," leading me to believe that any woman from that era is most likely no longer a virgin and has five adult children. So, to her deflower-er (okay, I made that word up, but you can't do much with "deflower"), you can come out of hiding now.

❖ **Utah**: *A man is responsible for any criminal act committed by his wife while she is in his presence.* Now *that* we can work with. If hubby cheats on you, you can run over his mistress in your Durango, and, as long as he was there when it happened, *he's* responsible. It's what we call a "two-fer."

❖ **Massachusetts**: *A woman cannot be on top in sexual activities.* I'm not sure how anyone would actually know where either of you were positioned while you were getting your freaky on, but, after age fifty, women have taken care of that problem. (Why? Lay a mirror on the floor, and kneel down over it on all fours. Look down. Gravity at its peak, baby. Neither hubby nor law enforcement will ever see you in that position again.)

❖ **Georgia**: *Donkeys may not be kept in bathtubs.* I'm baffled as to why you'd have a donkey and what the hell it would be doing in your bathtub, but you need to know that this will not be tolerated in the great state of Georgia.

❖ **Michigan**: *Public indecency is generally not tolerated but is not actually illegal if it's on your property.* Specifically, if you want to have sex in your car, it must be performed in your driveway. Which explains all the cars going up and down like kids' bouncy castles in the neighborhood every night after 10 p.m.

❖ **New Mexico**: *Woman may walk around in public topless, provided they have their nipples covered.* Since they don't regulate what qualifies as "nipple coverage," I'm just going to use my belt, since that's where my nipples usually hang out.

And my all-time fave…

❖ **Texas**: *Criminals are required to give their victims twenty-four-hours' notice, either orally or in writing, explaining the nature of the crime they're going to commit against them.* (How can you not *love* this one??) "Hello, Mrs. Obermeyer? This is Ted. Remember, your plumber? Me and a few of my homeboys are coming over tomorrow night to boost that cool, seventy-inch flat screen you and hubby just bought. Yeah, we should be there about nine, so, if you two could maybe go to dinner or something so none of us get hurt, that would be super. Sound good to you?" It didn't address whether or not the victim is legally required to reply, but I think that would be the polite thing to do.

"You'd be surprised how much it costs to look this cheap."

~ Dolly Parton

Middle Age.
I'm Going to Need a Second Job

I WATCHED a TV reality show a few weeks ago that congratulated a woman on winning a "Total Beauty Makeover." She was apparently the homeliest one of the contestants, and the judges decided she was most in need of a complete overhaul. (And, of course, it would be the most dramatic, which is always good for ratings.)

At the end of the show, there was a giant blowup of her "Before" photo, used as a backdrop as she walked out onto the stage, beaming with smiles, flashing her perfect, white teeth, and tossing her shiny, newly blonde hair (complete with extensions) while wearing a wildly expensive outfit (including stilettos) that, I'm assuming, she plans to wear every day for the rest of her life.

Then they brought up a new backdrop that showed what the makeover cost. Oh. My. God.

My mother always said that the difference between a beautiful woman and a plain one was either God or a ton of money. Well, what God didn't give this woman, she bought (or won) for herself.

This got me thinking about how much women can spend trying to look "better." Thinner, prettier, *younger*. We live in a society that defines beauty, first and foremost, by *youth*, and the further it slips away, the more we're willing to spend to get it back.

Flipping through several women's magazines at a local drugstore, I mentally tabulated the fashion styles or beauty products they were pushing to midlifers who wanted to look younger. It's a zillion-dollar industry. It became obvious that Boomers don't balk at higher price points, if said products actually *do* what they advertise. And, with every passing decade, the gap gets wider between what we'll spend on ourselves when we're young and naturally perky, and what it costs us to stay that way when we're…, well, not.

> **Jeans then**: $20. Levi's 501 button-up. *Everybody* wore them. The Ray Ban of jeans. Cool factor, off the charts.
> **Jeans now**: $145. They need to fit our mature curves, boost our sagging butts, and flatten our post-baby bellies, all without smooshing everything over the top like a giant banana-nut muffin at Starbucks.

> **Shoes then**: $19 at Ross. Sexy, fabulous, killer heels. Uncomfortable as hell, but we looked so good, we didn't care.
> **Shoes now**: $120, with cushioned insoles and arch support, in low heels or flats. Stilettos are reserved for the bedroom. During the day, we need *comfort*, dammit. Especially on that side with the bunion.

> **Handbags then**: $39 for knock-off Kate Spades or Louis Vuittons. We own six. Our friends don't know for sure, and we're not telling.
> **Handbags now**: $400+ for one authentic Coach bag that we carry *everywhere*. Girlfriends know at a glance, and we're too old to pretend.

➢ **Underwear then**: $8 at Target for a three-stack of lacy panties and $10 a piece for matching bras designed to hold up two Chiclets that could stay up on their own accord.

Underwear now: $85 at Nordstrom for industrial-strength bras with Kevlar underwire that can hoist those babies up where belong. $78 at Spanx for tiny spandex tourniquets designed to compress, flatten, and reposition recalcitrant body parts that have gone rogue from gravity and questionable lifestyle choices.

➢ **Bathing suits then**: $19 for a tiny tube top and a brightly colored piece of dental floss to tie around our perky hips. We're Bo Derek, running on the beach in a bikini, still firm enough that our boobs don't flop out and whack us in the face, and the imperceptible jiggle in our butts is still considered hot.

Bathing suits now: *You're kidding*, right? $75 for mom-shorts, a tank top for tanning, an oversize straw hat, and a white shirt to pull on if we're actually going to ever get up off the chaise to go to the bathroom, lest anyone see our flying squirrel underarms, the cellulite on our thighs, or our belly pouch.

➢ **Hair care then**: $20 for the Herbal Essences combo-pack of shampoo, conditioner, and hair gel. $10 for pink leopard blow dryer from Claire's.

Hair care now: $59 for a three-month supply of Rogaine for Women. $42 for shampoo and conditioner to restore color-treated hair. $30 for gel and styling paste to make hair look fuller and shinier. $60 for ginormous blow dryer that filters "ions" and protects aging hair from falling out entirely. $89 every six weeks for hair stylist to revive our faded hair color and hide the gray, while still looking "natural."

> **Skin care then**: $20 for Proactive Kit or Neutrogena cleanser and lightweight moisturizer.
> **Skin care now**: $40 for cleanser and exfoliator. $60-$100 for moisturizer that promises to tighten, brighten, lift, nourish, and renew our tired, middle-aged faces. $75 for the serum to put *under* the moisturizer because it can apparently only do so much and we need concentrated help. $18 for sunscreen during the day. $87 for collagen-boosting night cream, because we'll believe anything. $400 for quarterly Botox session to remove what our $90 moisturizer couldn't fix.

> **Body care**: $15 for soap, deodorant, and toothpaste.
> **Body care now**: $55 for soap, in-shower body exfoliator (that dead skin doesn't slough itself anymore), body lotion for dry or damaged skin, and deodorant. $12 for whitening toothpaste (more red wine, anyone?), $400 for whitening trays from the dentist, and $50/month for bleaching gel to put into the whitening trays.

> **Makeup then**: $18 for tinted moisturizer. $25 for a cute kit at Sephora that includes mascara, lip gloss, four eyeshadows, liner, and blusher. With brushes.
> **Makeup now**: $60 for anti-aging foundation. $140 for eyelash growth serum. $60 for eyeshadows and blushers that don't look like a child's glitter craft project. $25 for thickening mascara. $35 for lipstick and matching liner, because we no longer have lip lines. $18 for eyebrow pencil, to put back what we've been plucking out every morning for the last forty-five years.

> **Tanning then**: $40 for a summer pass to local tanning bed. $3 for tanning bed protective goggles. $8 for tanning oil accelerator.

> **Tanning now**: $26 for 30+ SPF sunscreen for face and body. $48 for "natural" spray-on tan that doesn't streak. (And, actually, we're less interested in the actual tan than the knowledge that tan fat looks better than white fat.)

And we wonder why we're always broke.

The other morning, Hubs suggested we get up and go look at houses we might want to buy. I told him to give me an hour or two, because I was cruising the want ads for a second job. We either need more income or less outgo. Maybe he'll consider a yurt.

"For what do we live, but to make sport for our neighbors and laugh at them in our turn?"

~ Jane Austen

The Neighbors. They Like Us.
Really, They Do

FOR SEVERAL years, Hubs and I owned a lovely little house at the end of a tree-lined street. It wasn't big or particularly expensive, but it sat on a large lawn with a row of giant fir trees on one side, creating a shaded, park-like setting where we hosted roughly a thousand BBQs, countless summer family gatherings, and our son's wedding.

But, as the years went by, we began to feel that the house owned *us*. Remodeling, repairing, updating, and preventative maintenance seemed never-ending. I took care of the inside of the house, and Hubs was in charge of all things yard-, garden-, or car-related.

He had a reputation around the neighborhood for being *extremely* fastidious about his lawn. Neighbors would walk by and point out a nonexistent clover in the yard, just to watch Hubs scream, "*WHERE*??" Weeds, moles, clover, or any other flaws were simply not allowed. I was the same way about the inside. Not surprisingly, we were always exhausted. And perpetually broke.

Eventually, like many Boomers, we decided to downsize to a place that didn't require all the energy of a cracked-out squirrel (a *well-to-do*, cracked-out squirrel) to keep it maintained. We decided to sell the house and move into a cute rental that had everything we needed. Life was good.

Then Hubs came home one night and grinned, "Our old house is for sale. The neighbors said it doesn't look the same, and they want us to buy it back. Seems we were good for property values."

"But why would the new owners want to sell it? They've only been there for a couple of years," I asked.

He laughed. "Because the people who bought it figured out how much work it took to make it look like it did when they bought it. Seems *they* aren't dumb enough to spend their days picking clover out of the yard with tweezers. *We* were absolutely that dumb, which the neighborhood loved. And it seems they also thought we were entertaining."

My mind did a quick replay of what those neighbors had witnessed over the years, and I wasn't sure if we should buy back our house, change our names, and move to another state, or stay where we were and write a book called *How to Be a Good Neighbor (Even When You're Naked),* to be given out at the next block Christmas party.

We spent the rest of the evening laughing over a bottle of wine, and remembering…

❖ One day, I bought one of those stupid bras that claimed to be "five bras in one." Halter, strapless, whatever. Obviously invented by a man whose fantasy woman was a double-jointed circus contortionist. I spent half an hour trying to figure out the straps, then another half hour sweating it up, trying to get into it. I finally got so frustrated, I threw it out the bedroom window. It landed smack in the middle of Old Man Brisby's arborvitae. I never retrieved it. And he's never mentioned it.

❖ One spring, Hubs was replacing all the woodwork inside the house and needed a dumpster to toss the old wood out. Fully aware that I'm congenitally incapable of backing up a car in a straight line, he parked the dumpster *directly behind my car*. Backing out, I freaked when I suddenly saw it in my rear-view mirror. I cranked a hard right and miraculously managed to miss it by a couple of inches. I didn't, however, miss Mrs. Wagonbottom's prizewinning cat's tail. Unsure about the proper etiquette for that particular situation, I offered to buy her a whole new cat (quickly discovering Mrs. W had *zero* sense of humor). It took months for her to feel the love again, and her cat still hisses at me whenever I walk by.

❖ Soon after that, I decided to focus on hiding the evidence of my back-up fails (often evidenced by flattened grass trails that instantly announced "She was *here*"). I bought a rake to get the grass nap going the right way again. Good idea, until Mr. McNosy Pants next door saw Hubs and called out, "Hey, I saw your wife drive over your yard, then get out of her car and rake the wet grass. What was she *doing*??" When I got home, my rake was leaning up against the front door, with a note that said: *Anything you want to tell me?* (A week later, I read an article about getting rid of moles by redirecting them to burrow in another direction. Like, say, to the neighbor's house. Turns out it's actually pretty simple. But I swear it wasn't me.)

❖ Home one summer night, and not in the mood for TV, Hubs jumped up, opened the front door, and cranked up some old time rock-and-roll for a little living room dancing. We were enthusiastically busting our admittedly goofy middle-age dance moves, which used to mortify our kids, when we looked out the large front window to see the usually reserved couple from down the street doing a mean swing dance in our driveway. They left laughing, shouting out, "Thanks for the dance!" It was a rare moment of neighborly bonding with these two. And the next Christmas, when Hubs put his twelve-foot blinking snowman on the roof, they didn't say a word.

❖ On a warm, spring day, Hubs was tackling a big lawn project while I was in the shower. He slid open the bedroom window and called out, "Come see!"

"Um, I'm in the shower. Can it wait?"

"Just grab a towel," he said. "It will only take a second."

Hmmm. So far the neighbors had seen me cave in the garage ceiling, chase my Chihuahua down the street in my bathrobe, repeatedly rear-end anything Hubs put behind my car, and mow down three mailboxes, trying to get the mail without getting out of my car. The one shred of dignity I had left was that they hadn't yet seen me running across the yard in a towel, high-fiving Hubs for his gardening efforts. But what the hell? Dignity is overrated.

I grabbed a towel and sprinted into a fairly impressive fifty-yard dash across the lawn and back. The neighborhood grapevine later reported that Mrs. Wagonbottom told Mr. Wagonbottom she's not exactly sure what she saw, but it appeared to be a naked woman wearing only a towel running across our yard. He thinks it's her meds.

And my favorite:

❖ On most warm nights, my little convertible is parked outside in the driveway. I got up one morning and it was gone. I raced down the hall, yelling, "I think my car got stolen last night!!"

"No, it didn't." Hubs yawned. "It rained last night, so I got up around three to pull it into the garage."

"You got up and got dressed just to put my car away?"

"Nope," he said. "It was raining so hard, I didn't have time. So I just ran out there naked and hopped in."

OMG.

"Now the neighbors don't think *either* of us ever wears clothes," I pointed out.

"Yeah." He laughed. "But they'll miss us when we're gone."

Apparently, they actually do.

"*A man without a smiling face must not open a shop.*"

~ Chinese Proverb

Customer Service.
You're Doing it Wrong

A FEW DAYS ago, during yet another frustrating computer malfunction, I called Dell's "Award-Winning Service Department" and got Akbar in Sri Lanka, who sounded eager to try out his new online diploma in English-as-a-ninth-language. He announced that, before we could proceed with my questions, he needed to access my account. We spent the next twenty minutes trying to spell Claflin. ("C as in cat. No, not *bat*. L, I, F. No, not S. *F* as in *Frank.* Another I, N as in Nancy. Not M—*N*." Repeat nine times.)

By the time I was ready to slam my head into the wall, he sighed and said, "Well, it seems your warranty has expired, so I'll need your credit card. It's forty dollars to talk to our Tech department."

"But what if they can't help me?" I asked.

"Then there's no additional charge," he replied. "The $40 is just to transfer the call."

Some days, you just want to smack someone.

Having taught classes in customer service during the late '70s and early '80s, I admit that my bar is probably unrealistic, especially when the customer service department is located in another country or in stores where the merchandise is displayed in shrink-wrapped boxes stacked six deep on wooden pallets. And I'm not asking for a personal shopper to greet me at the door with champagne and chocolates (although it's a hell of a marketing idea). But I'm constantly amazed at how often rudeness, apathy, or ignorance appear to be part of the job description for customer service positions.

Over the years, I've mentally collected a few particularly outstanding, cringe-worthy customer service fails, forever seared into my brain as the "best of the worst" responses I've heard.

+ **Me:** "Do you carry the Magic Bra Genie that fits every woman, regardless of bra size?"

Salesclerk (continuing to fold a huge pile of sweaters and pointing to a vague geographical region in a 150,000-square-foot store): "I'm not sure. But *if* we had it, it would be over there."

Okay, then. I'll just go spend another hour or so looking around the Back 40 by myself. Do you want me to come back and let you know if you carry it?

ଦ୍ୱଦ୍ୱ

+ **Me:** "Do you carry these jeans?"

Salesclerk: "Their not really in style anymore, so, no, we don't. Have you tried Goodwill?"

Yeah, that's always my first choice when I'm looking for new clothes.

+ After spending thirty minutes with the Help Desk and not fixing the problem, "Is there anything else we can do for you?"

Anything *else*?? You haven't done anything *yet*.

ଦ୍ୱଦ୍ୱ

+ **Me:** "I'm looking for this lipstick in 'Hey, Sailor Red.'"

Saleswoman: "Oh, we get asked for that *all the time*, but we don't carry it."

Why not??

ଓ଼ଓ଼

+ **Me:** "I'd like this skirt in a size 8."

Saleswoman: "Really, sweetie? You look more like a 12. But we don't go that big. Do you still want to try the 8?"

While I'm deciding, lean in a little closer so I can slap you.

ଓ଼ଓ଼

+ **Me:** "May I get the check, please?"

Server: "Here you go. And I applied your senior discount."

So, you just assumed I was a senior, since you're, like, what, twelve?? Here's your tip: Ask next time.

ଓ଼ଓ଼

+ **Me:** "I love this dress. What do you think?"

Saleswoman: "You could totally wear that. You just need some Spanx to smooth out those bumps."

You mean I could rock this if I didn't have those unfortunate butt lumps and belly fat? Yeah, let's just girdle the crap out of those areas. I feel sexy now.

+ **Me:** "How's the linguini here?"

Server: "I don't know. I've never had it, because I don't personally like the way the sauce looks. But we sell a lot of it, so it's probably okay."

Thanks, but I'll just have another glass of wine and a breadstick.

ᏩᎸᏛ

❦ **Me:** "I need to return this handbag. It's not going to work for me."

Salesclerk: "Oh, we don't do that."

Me: "Why not?"

Salesclerk: "It's our *policy*."

Unless that policy came down on the Stone Tablets and was written by the Good Lord himself, I'm thinking you won't be struck by lightning if you get out a pen and *change* your stupid policy.

ᏩᎸᏛ

❦ **Me:** "My computer keeps shutting itself down. How do I fix that?"

Computer guy: "Well, it's working at *our* end, so I don't know what to tell you."

Well, it's your product. If *you* don't know, I'm pretty much screwed. What's the phone number of your competitor?

ᏩᎸᏛ

❦ After waiting twenty-five minutes in line at the in-store Help Desk, "I'm sorry, but there's nothing we can do for you."

Seriously, nothing? Not even a suggestion or a referral? A refund? A store credit? You've got *nothing*??

ᏩᎸᏛ

🜲 While waiting (and waiting and waiting) on hold for assistance, "Your call is very important to us. Please hold for the next available agent."

Color me stupid, but if my call is that important to you, you'd have someone to *answer* it. Every time that condescending message plays, I hate you just a little bit more.

⚬⚬

🜲 After twenty-five minutes in line at the grocery store, **Me:** "I don't think your register is accurate. Go-gurt had one of those sales stickies on it for half price."

Clerk: "Well, you're welcome to go back to where you found it and get the sales ticket and bring it back here."

Me: "But won't I have to wait in line again?"

She shrugged. "Guess so."

Few things leave me speechless...

⚬⚬

So I was shopping at Safeway the other day, in the early morning hours, and there was only one available checker. The lineup of shoppers snaked all the way back to Produce. The poor checker was completely frazzled but doing the best she could, while looking helplessly at the extended stream of increasingly cranky customers trying to get to work on time.

After a half hour of waiting through the inevitable price checks, coupon clippers, lost Safeway cards, and I-forgot-the-milk-be-right-backs, I finally got the chance to ask her *why* on earth she was all alone.

She replied, "They're all at Customer Service training."

Okay, that one was almost too easy.

"An open marriage is Nature's
way of saying
you need a divorce."

~ Ann Landers

8 Things That Can Tank Your Marriage

STATISTICS TELL us that over half of first marriages end in divorce. There's a divorce in the United States every thirty-six seconds. And over forty percent of marriages involve one or both parties guilty of infidelity. That number is generally acknowledged to be conservative because…, well, people lie.

What are we doing wrong? Has marriage become "going steady, with furniture"? Whenever we get bored or unhappy, do we just "break up" like middle-school tweeners and move on to newer, greener pastures at the local gym? Is it a nationwide epidemic of "Wedding Fever," where the couple puts ridiculous amounts of time and money into the ceremony but thinks the marriage should magically take care of itself? (Pay attention, Kardashian girls.)

It appears that no matter how much two people love each other, the odds of going the distance are not in their favor. We may never know all the reasons couples don't last, but we do know some of the most common.

1. **One of you saves; one of you spends**. Financial problems are considered by many marital experts to be the Big Kahuna wrecking ball to lasting happiness as a couple. If Hubby thinks tracking the return on his investments is the

most fun he has all day, but *you* insist that a cruise to the Bahamas with your besties is a quality-of-life issue, you two are headed for a smackdown. And if *he* uses the account you opened for three-year-old Bitsy's college fund to buy an expensive fishing boat, hopefully he left enough money for his extended stay at the local Shilo Inn.

2. **One of you wants it and one of you doesn't.** Yes, I'm talking about sex. If he's chasing you down the hall every night, wearing nothing but a smile and a stiffy, and you're more of a once-a-month-and-I'm-good type of woman, he might just give up and quit asking altogether. If you shimmy into a garter belt and push-up bra five nights a week, and all he wants to do is grab a beer and watch an hour or two of *Pawn Shop* before he hits the sack, eventually one of you is going to complain. Loudly.

3. **One of you feels like you "married up."** While this may be a little thrilling in the early stages, it's demeaning to constantly feel like your spouse is "out of your league." Maybe he has more education than you do. Maybe you come from a wealthy family and he doesn't. Whichever partner is experiencing this insecurity tends to get defensive and on guard for little slights. *He* says, "I don't think you'll like this wine." *You* hear, "You don't know anything about fine wine. Here's some ice. Make a spritzer." Or *you* say, "I wish we could go to Italy, but it's just not in the budget right now," and *he* hears, "You can't even make enough for a trip to Italy, you loser." You'll recognize these marriages when you see them. One of the spouses is always hurt or pissed off, and the other one just stands around looking confused.

4. **Addiction problems.** Whether it's alcohol, gambling, drugs, shopping, or any other option from a long list of emotional and pharmaceutical possibilities, addictions can

torpedo even the strongest marriages. It's extremely difficult to feel the love for Hubby after he lost your house in a crap game during a weekend guys' trip to Las Vegas. And his love for you may wane a tad when he begins to wonder if you're doing the UPS guy, because he's at your house every afternoon, smiling and bearing packages from your drunken midnight shopping binges on QVC.

5. **Crazy families**. He can't stand your mother. You hate his kids. His mom passed away and his aging father (the groper) is moving in with you. Your sister hit on him at last year's Christmas dinner, and she seems hell-bent on giving it another go this year. Families range from somewhat complicated to full-on freak shows, but we can't break up with them. He may have to learn to smile as your mother uses every conversation to remind you that Howard, the doctor, would have been able to take you to Italy. And you need to start sending his kids birthday gifts. On time. With a card.

6. **Best friends**. Both parties often bring BFFs into the relationship. But if he doesn't like Susie, your BFF since high school, and she's over *all the time*, he's going to start fencing off a Susie-free zone around the house perimeter. If his obnoxious college frat buddy regularly shows up unannounced, toting two six-packs, and plants himself on the couch with Hubby, where they spend the rest of the evening in raucous drinking, watching the Big Game and foraging through your refrigerator like Yogi and Boo Boo on crack, you might eventually end up moving to another state. Without the two of them.

7. **Unrealistic expectations**. This is more often seen in younger marriages. Young love is starry-eyed and all-consuming. The blissed-out couple believes their love is "special" and they'll be this enthralled by the other

person's breathing every single day. *Forever*. When that heart-stopping intensity wears off (and we get back to Real Life, before we're homeless, friendless, and unemployed), people often think the best part of their marriage is over. These couples constantly refer to their wedding as "the happiest day of their lives." We can only assume from that comment that it's all been downhill from there.

8. **Cheating.** There are thousands of books and articles on why people become cheaters. It's exciting. It's forbidden. You feel desirable again. To the "cheatee," it doesn't really matter *why*. It's just matters that you *did*. Tired clichés like "I never meant to hurt you" are stupid and grounds for matrimonial murder in thirty-eight states. And even worse, the proverbial "It was no big deal." So you're saying that you sacrificed our marriage for something that was totally meaningless to you?? Wow. I'd rather you left me for your soul mate. That's less insulting. Some marriages get through this one. Most don't.

Now, go hug your spouse.

"Frankly, I don't trust any diet that doesn't allow sugar."

~ Bethenny Frankel

Marriage & Dieting.
Sometimes It's a Team Sport

HUBS AND I have been married for seventeen years. Over that time, he has habitually told everyone he meets that he's learned a lot about women in those years. Apparently, his first two wives weren't what he refers to as girly-girls, so he came into our relationship with only a rudimentary understanding of the term "high maintenance."

Hubs has learned how many different shades of black there are for boots, why every bed requires a minimum of six throw pillows, and how a woman can be on a diet for fifteen years and never lose an ounce. *He* can cut back on late-night chip dip and knock off a quick eight pounds, while I'm down the hall charting the pros and cons of various weight-loss options and why *they never work*. Admittedly, I have a dieting attention span of approximately three hours. I've been on virtually every recognized diet on the planet (including a few that came with a warning label, "Do Not Do For More Than Three Days or You Will Die"; what the hell, I was young). But nothing seems to work. Apparently, I suck at dieting.

Whenever Hubs looks confused about yet another failed attempt to divest myself of the same ten pounds I've been battling since 1974, I explain to him, again, how the entire premise of dieting is just *wrong*. Diets work like budgets. They're both fundamentally about *deprivation*.

The first thing budget experts tell you to do is write down everything you like to spend money on. Then they get out their fat red markers and cross off all the "unnecessary things" you can't buy anymore. We've just reached our first crossroads.

I told our first fiscal planner, "If I could *resist* these things, I wouldn't *buy* them. In that case, I wouldn't need your advice. But since I *can't* resist them, there's no point in telling me I can't buy them, because I'm going to anyway, and now I'm a loser, but with fabulous boots." (Hubs thought I should add here that we're on our third accountant.)

Diet experts, similarly, tell you to write down all your favorite foods, and then tell you that you can never eat them again. *Ever*. Yeah, no. If I *liked* broccoli, I'd *eat* broccoli, in which case, I wouldn't need you and your stupid Acceptable Foods list. Since I hate broccoli and I love chocolate, here we are, back at Deprivation Gulch. Hubs claims that, after seventeen years, this makes a weird sort of sense to him. He's learning.

Meanwhile, the poor guy has vicariously lived through a multitude of failed programs with an admirable lack of judgment.

There was Weight Watchers. All that planning, counting, and cooking food I wasn't going to eat quickly devolving into a drive-by lobbing of their annoying Point Counter into the soccer field on my way to DQ for an Oreo Lava Blizzard.

He quietly sat through a short trial of Nutrisystem. Foil-wrapped space-shuttle food. Tried it once and gave the nonrefundable supply to Paco, my Chihuahua, who will eat anything. Except that.

Moving forward to Medifast. Hungry, all the time. And consequently, bitchy. All. The. Time.

And, of course, we tried low carb. By day three, I would have tossed Paco under a bus in a New York minute for a bagel. Not my best moment.

Finally, I ended up at Jenny Craig. No cooking, counting, meetings, or public weigh-ins. Simply pick out my favorite Jenny foods and *poof!* A month-long supply right to our door, all pre-packaged, actually edible, and ready to eat. Perfect. Hubs thought the portions looked a tad scant, and I almost lost him over the shipping and handling (fourteen boxes of frozen food, overnight express, from eight states away... Ouch). But I promised that, *this* time, I'd stay on it until the food was gone. Deal.

The UPS truck pulled up and we watched while box after box was unloaded and set on the porch. It quickly became obvious that Jenny was going to take up every square inch of our kitchen fridge and freezer. Hubs tried to be supportive, but he finally turned to me and stated flatly, "If I find *one* of those frozen boxes in my beer fridge, Jenny dies." Fair enough.

I lost thirteen pounds over the next three months. Then I quit eating Jenny food and gained it back in six weeks. Well, crap.

It was clear that programmed dieting was not for me, so Hubs suggested just making small, daily changes, on the premise that they would eventually add up and coax recalcitrant scale numbers to budge downward. It wouldn't be quick, but it could work.

Since my biggest struggle is giving up desserts, I started shopping for smaller portions of my favorites. But Sara Lee doesn't *sell* one cookie or one slice of cake. This often meant buying the smallest size available, eating enough to satisfy the original lust, and then throwing the rest away so I didn't pork it all down in one evening just because "it's there."

Shortly into my New Plan, a sweet attack sent me scurrying to the local bakery for one of those "individual size" German chocolate cakes (for 2+ individuals, but only if you share.

Bahahahaha). I gently warmed it up, ate what I wanted, and tossed the rest. As I walked away, I looked at Hubs proudly and said, "I've *so* got this down."

Until I got up the next morning.

He came into the kitchen while I was bent over, face in the garbage and butt in the air, and said, "I know I'm going to be sorry I asked, but *what are you doing*??"

I thought about lying and saying I was taking out the trash, but we've been married too long. What the hell. "I'm looking to see if my cake touched anything skeevy in here. If not, grab a fork, because we're getting it out of here."

"Oh, for God's sake," he replied. "Get your coat and we'll go buy you a new piece. And today, this diet sh** ends. Just eat the damn cake."

He so gets me.

"If someone ever asks you to do something for them, do it really bad so you never have to do it again."

~ Paris Hilton

If I'd Known Then What I Know Now

ONE OF MY clearest memories from high school was one afternoon, sitting in the library with a group of friends and chatting about what we imagined we'd be doing in the year 2000 (which, at that time, seemed a million years away).

Naturally, there were those over-achievers who said they'd be running the country through a well-paid political office (or, if they were class valedictorians, from the White House), curing cancer, or homeschooling their six adopted Russian children in their yurt. Others were a tad less aspirational but still admirable. They saw their older selves teaching inner-city kids or leading a church flock to salvation.

All I remember thinking was that I'd be forty-three and it wouldn't matter how I looked anymore. I could stop obsessing about my weight and toss my too-tight, junior-sized jeans and tiny cheerleading skirts forever. I'd live out my remaining days in giant floral muumuus from Hilo Hattie's, eating whatever I liked and simply tenting the thirty-five pounds I'd inevitably pack on as a result. At forty-three, I'd be past the age where it mattered. "Old age" had a clear upside. (Yes, I was shallow; I was also fifteen. But that's redundant.)

When I look back on that moment, it always makes me laugh. God, I knew *nothing* and didn't have a clue about life outside of high school. They say, "Youth is wasted on the young." I agree. I often wonder how different our lives might be, if we knew at twenty what we know at fifty. The possibilities of youth, combined with the wisdom of age. Would our priorities have been different? Would our relationships have been healthier? Would we have been better parents? Better partners? Followed our dreams earlier?

If I could go "back to the future" and talk to my teenage self, here are some things I wish I'd known then:

> **Whenever possible, ignore means girls and their posse.** At your twentieth class reunion, Bitsy will be living in a trailer park with four kids and a sporadically employed husband, spending her days in wine-infused walks down memory lane, when she was all that.

> **Stop comparing.** There will always be somebody younger, prettier, and thinner than you. And many of them will have more money. Comparisons just make us more competitive with other women, and, someday, we might need each other.

> **Be kind.** Even when there's nothing in it for you. Karma is real. And she can be a bigger bitch than you.

> **Learn to laugh at yourself.** If you don't, somebody else will. If you can't laugh at your foibles, you come across as a self-important douche with no sense of humor.

> **If you're not happy, it's your problem.** Fix your own crap. Everybody else has their own to work out. Don't expect them to work out yours.

> **Pick your battles.** Is this issue still going to be important in twenty years? If so, suit up and fight it out. If not, let it go. And, seriously, in fifty years, we'll all be dead and none of this will matter.

➢ **No matter how wonderful you are, there will be people who don't like you**. Cut them loose.

➢ **Forgive**. We're all human. We screw up. Accept apologies when offered, and then *forget about it*. You'll both be happier.

➢ **If you love someone, tell them**. Even if they don't say it back. Love is a gift, and nobody ever died from being too generous.

➢ **Share**. If you have something that could make another person's journey a little easier, share it. Trust that it will come back to you in ways you might not even imagine. You don't need to keep score. The universe has a wonderful way of balancing the scales. (See #3.)

➢ **Learn from your mistakes** and let go of what you "could have done better." Learn something and do it better next time.

➢ **Make yourself a priority**. Letting your loved ones run you ragged, sacrificing your mental and physical health to make sure they're comfy and happy every minute of every day does not make you a good person. It makes you a doormat.

➢ **Chasing a goal can be as much fun as achieving it**. Enjoy the process.

➢ **You'll worry less about what people think of you if you realize how seldom they do.**

➢ **If you don't ask, you don't get**. Even the people who love you can't read your mind.

➢ What's the #1 rule of negotiation? **Figure out what's in it for the other guy**. (Believe it or not, he doesn't always care what works for *you*.) If you can do this, you can achieve world peace.

➤ **Never let fear of failure hold you back**. Trying is half the fun, and failure makes for great stories at a party. People will always be more interested in your failures than your successes.

➤ **Surround yourself with people who love you, who encourage you, and who celebrate who you are**. If they criticize, judge, or belittle you, they're gone.

➤ **Be good to the people you love**. We're all busy. Take the time to give back. The world is full of old, lonely people who never took the time or gave back to the people who loved them. And now, nobody does.

➤ **Consider carefully what you're chasing**. Eternal youth? Not possible. Money? May cost you more than it's worth. Fame? Fleeting, at best.

➤ **Be the first to say "I'm sorry."** Even if they're wrong. Sometimes, you have to choose between being right and having a relationship with this person. Choose wisely.

➤ **Happiness is a decision**. "Most folks are as happy as they make up their minds to be." (And life is just more *fun*, if you're happy.)

➤ Remember, **no matter what you're going through, just breathe**. This, too, shall pass.

"My heart says chocolate and wine,
but my jeans say,
'For the love of God, woman, eat a salad.'"

~ Unknown

Jeans Shopping.

The Reason God Invented Yoga Pants

STOP THE FIRST ten women you meet in the street and ask them for their least favorite clothes-shopping item. Eight of them will say "swimsuits." But, bikinis aside (since most boomers haven't tried one on since 1989), even expensive, well-cut, one-piece swimsuits have a way of outing our last dozen diet failures and the 1,496 times we *didn't* get to the gym in the last decade.

But, in most cases, any onesie from Miraclewear or Spanx, if purchased in our actual size and not the size we keep telling ourselves we wear, will provide enough boob lift, butt coverage, and belly flattening spandex to get us from our hotel room to poolside with minimal assault on our self-esteem. If all else fails, there's always the beloved sarong cover-up. Classy, and covers up everything from the waist down. *Definitely* invented by a woman.

But jeans? That's a different problem altogether. Let's start with the fact that jeans were not originally designed for women. Especially women with curves. They were created for *men*. Yes, that species with bodies that go straight up and down. Calves, thighs, hips, and waist, all approximately the same circumference, with a body shape more rectangular than hourglass. (I know there are women who are built like that: mile-long legs, slim hips, and tiny little waists. Just to be clear, I hate those women, and we will never be friends. My therapist says I have issues. I'm thinking the fact that I *have* a therapist pretty much covers that.)

For those of us with bodies more reminiscent of the soft, squishy curves of Play-Doh than the relentlessly straight angles of Legos, jeans can be a shopping nightmare.

Most women are a minimum of two different sizes, and that's just from the waist down. We need to factor in waist size, hip circumference, and leg length. A waist that is one size, a butt that's another, and inseam measurements that range from French bulldog to gazelle can all make jeans-sizing almost worthless.

My experience? If the jeans fit my waist, the hips feel like they're wrapped in an Ace bandage. If they fit through the hips, you could stick three friends in the waistband. With a long torso, *every* style is a low-rider, whether they're labeled that way or not. I struggled with visible butt crack before anyone but the local plumber knew what it was. Needless to say, when I find a pair of jeans that fit, I wear them until they fall off.

With this knowledge, and not-so-little trepidation, I found myself at Nordstrom, needing a new pair of jeans. I explained my predicament to the perky young saleswoman, and she smiled brightly.

"I'm Priscilla. And of *course* I can help you. So, a size 6?"

(Having been in retail for a thousand-plus years, I'm fully aware that you *always* suggest the next number down, when guessing a woman's size. Get that one wrong and your commission just charged out the door in a huff, never to return.)

"Actually, I'm an 8," I replied.

"Well, you look like a 6," she chirped, "but let me see what we have in an 8." Oh, Prissy was good.

She deposited me in the plush dressing room and returned shortly with more jeans than I've purchased collectively in my lifetime, handing them to me one at a time, so I could try them on at my leisure, "without getting overwhelmed" (read: suicidal), in case nothing worked. Yep, young Priscilla was a pro.

The first pair was dark-wash low-riders. Loved the deep blue color, but I'm built like a Welsh Corgi: long body, short legs. "Low-rise" on me means below my butt crack. I don't even have to bend over or squat down to display my backside hoo-ha, in all its sixty-year-old glory, to people who don't need to see it, ever. Some things are just cosmically *wrong*. Next?

Over the door came the traditional nightmare (Levi's 501s, anybody?). Good fit through the thighs but cut off the circulation in my hips and had my waist oozing over the top like an exploding Hot Pocket. These were promptly launched back over the door and replaced by a pair that fit comfortably through the hips, but the waist kept sliding down and the legs were baggy. I felt like a middle-aged Justin Bieber.

Then she tossed over a pair of soft blue denim with a textured, brocade-type swirl, "just for fun." Good fit, but I couldn't stop thinking about Scarlett's drapes from *Gone with the Wind*. Nope.

Next came skinny jeans. We could have stopped right there, but Prissy was not budging until I agreed to *try*. They required some rigorous hopping and pulling to get them up past my thighs and would only button if I lay flat on my back and exhaled to flatten my tummy (shades of my college days). Since I'm too old to get dressed on the floor (and it takes too long to get up), back over the door they sailed.

Our next option looked pretty good but had enough bling on the ass to work as reflective gear and help bring planes to the tarmac. And, of all my body parts I don't want to light up like a Las Vegas stripper, it would be *that*. Keep trying, Miss Priss.

Just as I was ready to concede defeat and hit the closest wine bar for a bottle of cheap cabernet and a good cry, she opened the door ever-so-slightly and stuck her hand in, holding a pair of soft, narrow-legged, higher-waisted jeans in a gorgeous charcoal color, rolled up at the cuffs, with just the right amount of seriously cool, rocker chick distressing. OMG. They were *perfect.* No butt crack cleavage, fitted through the hips, curved in at the waist, with just a touch of spandex to keep everything from jiggling when I was standing still. They had three colors in my size. I bought them all.

I gave Priscilla a hug and got her private number into my speed-dial for future shopping trips. Then I loaded up my bounty and happily headed for the closest wine bar. This time, I'm ordering the good stuff.

"I do not believe in using women in combat, because females are too fierce."

~ Margaret Mead

If Women Ruled the World

I CAME ACROSS that quote one day, and it instantly had me laughing out loud. My brain began writing an essay even before I rushed down the hall to my office.

After much not-so-serious thought and a few hilarious phone calls to girlfriends whom I knew would have instant contributions, here's my picture of what life would be like if women ruled the world.

- ❖ **A good glass of wine would cost no more than a beer.** Just because you can't belch it, doesn't mean it needs to be twice the price.

- ❖ **Women's haircuts would cost no more than a man's.** My hair and Hubs's are roughly the same length. His price, $14. Mine, $42. Equal pay is pointless, if we're not being equally charged for services.

- ❖ **It would be illegal for fashion designers and photographers to use pre-pubescent twizzle sticks to model their clothes.** Real-size, adult models or no runway show for you, buddy.

- ❖ **Makeup would be optional.** Always.

- ❖ **Store mannequins would include sizes 8-14.** And in regular department stores, not just "plus-size" boutiques.

- ❖ **Yoga pants would be acceptable attire anywhere.** You'd never again hear us say, "I'm not going. I don't have anything to wear."

- ❖ **Women's jeans would cost the same as men's.** His jeans, $48. Mine, $180. And his are often more flattering than mine. What's wrong with this picture??

- ❖ **Stilettos would only be sold in the lingerie department**, as bedroom wear, and shoe designers would be required to include fabulous flats as part of their line. Roughly half the female population doesn't wear stilettos at work. Keep up, shoe people.

- ❖ **Fluorescent lights would be banned from all offices and retail stores.** Soft lighting or pink tones would be standard in all offices and retail dressing rooms. And, if you're selling swimsuits, we expect a dimmer switch.

- ❖ **All scales would be calibrated at the manufacturing site to display five pounds less.** We won't tell if you don't.

- ❖ **Health insurance would be required to cover massages, housekeeping services, and wine tasting in lieu of therapy.** I'm sixty. I don't need prenatal care.

- ❖ **Fashion designers would have to manufacture their new lines in a full range of sizes**, including those over size 12. I know it's adorable in a size 2, but we can't all fit into an adult onesie. Get real, you guys.

- ❖ **All gas stations would be manned by gas jockeys** (no more self-serve crap), preferably hired from the Chippendale company.

❖ **Men who slept around would be considered tramps, while a woman who did the same would be applauded for her social skills**. It requires a lot of finesse to take out every guy in your office. You go, girl.

❖ **All firemen would look like the guys in the calendars**. Men want us to look like *Sports Illustrated* swimsuit models. Is this too much to ask?

❖ **If you slept with your boss and you got fired, so would he**. What a concept.

❖ **Women would be paid the same as men for any job**. No exceptions. Duh.

❖ *More* **magazine would have an annual swimsuit edition, with male models in banana hammocks**. Yep, guys, we're visual, too.

❖ **Grocery stores would deliver 24/7**. Including wine. We'd tip. We'd tip good.

❖ **Bars would check men for wedding-ring tan lines upon entry**, and provide loaners, if he "forgot" his own. Better yet, they'd call his wife.

❖ **Restaurants would offer the dessert menu first**. If we're still hungry, we'll order dinner.

❖ **Once a year, men would make chocolate and wine trays for us, while we group binge on** *The Good Wife*. After fourteen years of all the weenie wraps, chips & clam dip bowls, and half-time beer runs we've made for you on Game Day, this seems fair.

❖ **Hiking up to the third-floor wine bar at Nordstrom would be considered exercise**. It's three floors. With shopping bags.

- ❖ **Height and weight charts would be calculated by women** and allow for age, childbirth, and menopause, thus eliminating all guilt over those "last fifteen pounds."

- ❖ **The DMV would offer at least two choices of photographs for your license.** If we have our eyes closed or we look tired, we want a do-over.

- ❖ **Cookies would never add more weight to your body than they weigh in your hand.** Simple math.

- ❖ **Toilets would never flush while you're still seated.** One should never be scared of one's toilet.

- ❖ **Dressing rooms would always have a mirror *inside* the room.** We're tired of having to stand in the middle of the store in clothes that are too small, too tight, or that hang our back fat out for the public viewing.

- ❖ **Mammograms would be performed without having to flop our boobs onto a metal plate and then smash them with a vice.** We've never known a man who had to slap his weenie onto a piece of cold metal and then vice-grip it to check for abnormalities. There's got to be a better way.

- ❖ **Men would memorize "Have you lost weight?" "What other woman? You're the only woman in the room," and "I'm sorry, I won't do it again"** as standard, unwavering responses to most of our questions.

- ❖ **Men would go through menopause, with hot flashes, sweats, and mood swings.** We'd get the midlife crisis, the new Corvette, and the hot young trophy date.

- ❖ **There would never be more than a ten-year age gap between a leading man and a leading woman** in any movie.

❖ Media news stories about important men would start with a critique of his last haircut.

❖ Men would no longer believe that their cars and careers take work, but their marriages will maintain themselves.

❖ Overweight men would have to shop at plus-size stores. "Hilo Harry's, Men's Muumuus & More" would be the go-to spot for chubby hubbies.

❖ Spanx would introduce a men's line that all men, other than twenty-something Hollywood hunks, would be required to wear, so we wouldn't be subjected to their droopy man boobs and belly jiggle.

Utopia has arrived.

Did You Forget Your Free Gift?

SIGN UP for my mailing list to get updates on book releases, cover reveals, and other fun stuff, and never miss a post!

As a Thank You, I'll send you my *Ninja Closet Cleaning Course (What to Toss, What to Keep)*, and show you how to love your clothes again! It's one of my most-requested articles, and it's reserved only for subscribers.

Simply go to http://laugh-lines.net/, enter your name and email address, then click "DOWNLOAD NOW" for instant access.

It's fun, and it's FREE!

(I'll never share your name or email address, nor will I spam you.)

More Praise for CHIN HAIRS & BACK FAT

"Sitting here in my comfy sweats, and the worst cold I've had since I fit into a size six, with tissues, Theraflu, and Vikki Claflin's new book. I know many writers, and I've represented and managed comedians, but when it comes to humor that resonates with Baby Boomer women, Claflin takes the prize. The perfect gift for all the women 'of a certain age' on your list!"

Barbara Hammond,
The Psychic Way, Fine Tuning Your Intuition

"Warning: If your bladder control isn't what it used to be, strap on some Depends before reading, cause you're gonna laugh, hard. Right out of the gate, Claflin targets aging like a hot flash seeking missile. As my mother used to say, "The Golden Years Suck," but they suck less if you take Vikki Claflin with you!"

~ Kathleen O'Donnell, *The Last Day for Rob Rhino*

"Claflin once again delights readers with this charming and witty compilation of insights that only a mature kick-ass woman could envision. This book is for every card-carrying member of Club 50 and beyond who has ever needed reassurance that she is not alone. There's a feisty tribe of soulmates out there, and Claflin is a leader extraordinaire."

~ Kim Dalferes, *Magic Fishing Panties*

"If laughter is the best medicine, then Vikki Claflin's *Chin Hairs & Back Fat* is Xanax for the soul."
~ Linda Maltz Wolff, carpoolgoddess.com

"This is a definite must-read for any woman over 40. Vikki Claflin knows how to take the embarrassing facts, the personal stories, and the times you'd rather forget, and tell them to you like she was your best friend, with wit and humor abounding!! This is no normal comedy fiction. This is true life. If you don't laugh your pants off, you need another glass of wine!"
~ Jodie Filogomo, jtouchofstyle.com

"You know when you giggle at the Table of Contents in Vikki Claflin's new book that you're in for a laugh-fest throughout. Claflin's commentary on life after 60 not only rings true, but puts a hilarious spin on embarrassing situations we all experience. Pour yourself a glass of wine and enjoy this book. And share it with your girlfriends. They'll love you for it."
~ Helene Cohen Bludman, booksiswonderful.com

"Vikki's Claflin's midlife tell-all dishes up the sometimes-disconcerting reality of aging with a generous side of hilarious. Vikki inhabits our lives and reminds us that laughter and a nice glass of wine are the best antidotes to our aging woes."
~ Hélène Stelian, life coach and midlife expert
Next Act for Women

"A pure masterpiece! This book is what life is all about. Good laughs, fond memories and tips that may just save your life (especially the men out there). Sit back, relax, pick up all your body parts that are dragging on the floor, and dive head first into this "coming of age" tale. You won't regret it."
~ Michael Mele, the-insane-asylum.blogspot.com

"Vikki Claflin will be your new best friend after she humors you with this hilarious and brutally honest look at life after age 60. With anecdotal advice and wit, she encourages Boomers to seduce their hubbies with romantic comedies, accept the reality of fat pants, and forget the frivolous worries from their youth so they can enjoy more freedom to laugh."

~ Elaine Ambrose, *Midlife Happy Hour and Midlife Cabernet*

"Vikki's Claflin's midlife tell-all dishes up the sometimes-disconcerting reality of aging with a generous side of hilarious. Vikki inhabits our lives and reminds us that laughter and a nice glass of wine are the best antidotes to our aging woes."

~ Hélène Stelian, life coach and midlife expert
Next Act for Women

"Vikki Claflin's newest book is a funny, truthful, no-holds-barred look at the journey of life, and - more importantly - how to get around all the sucky parts of it. Heartfelt and humorous, Vikki's perspective proves to be a great how-to manual that everyone should read!"

~ Rodney Lacroix, *Romantic as Hell*

"Wow, just wow! Is Vikki Claflin living in my closet? She has humorously articulated many of my thoughts since becoming part of the "Big Girl Panties Society" from her previous book! Claflin's astute reflections on marriage and relationships are so helpful, I've posted them on my Facebook page, and on the bulletin board outside my office. Keep up the good work, Vikki!"

~ Anne Penniston Gray BA, BSW, RSW (SK),
Clinical Social Worker

"Vikki Claflin captures the heart and soul of being 60 in her new book. Give yourself the gift of laughter and belonging, and read this book. You'll walk away wanting Vikki as your neighbor, and with a deep sense of the value that comes with age."

~ Kimberly Montgomery, fiftyjewels.com

"I LOVED *Chin Hairs & Back Fat*. This book spoke *to* me, not at me. It felt like a conversation that made me laugh, think, and feel good about myself and aging. I cannot recommend this book highly enough. Whether for you, or someone you love, you will not go wrong buying Vikki Claflin's new book. We need more Vikkis in the world right now."

~ Michelle Combs, rubbershoesinhell.com

"With each passing birthday, I am more and more grateful for women like Vikki Claflin, who have the talent to bless us with the ability to look honestly in the mirror and appreciate not only where we've been but where we are going, and to laugh out loud on our way."

~ Doreen McGettigan, *Bristol-boyz Stomp;
The Stranger In My Recliner*

"I laughed aloud even as I perused the chapter titles, like 'From Cougar to Crazy Cat Lady - Has it Happened to You?' This book instantly resonates with me - it's funny, told warmly, sisterly - and reminds me we're all aging together, so we might as well do it gracefully and with humor! An instant pick-me-upper!"

~ Laura Sidsworth, *Spoiled Pink and The Treehouse Treasury*

"Vikki Claflin is BACK with another set of hysterical anecdotes, relatable stories, and heartwarming moments for our pleasure. Cleverly crafting the learning of a lifetime into humor gold, at heart, gorgeous messages of learning to love yourself and others with a bit more understanding and kindness. Thoroughly enjoyable!"

~ Lizzi Lewis, considerings.com

"Humorist Vikki Claflin's newest collection of stories will make you laugh out loud as she speaks candidly about midlife, marriage, friends and most importantly, her husband, the Hubs. She shares relatable stories that most of us are too embarrassed to repeat. Her wit and insight make her the friend you wish lived across the street."

~ Stacey Gustafson, *Are You Kidding Me? My Life With an Extremely Loud Family, Bathroom Calamities, and Crazy Relatives*

About Vikki

VIKKI CLAFLIN is an international best-selling author, humor blogger, and inspirational public speaker. She lives in Hood River, OR, where she writes the award-winning humor blog *Laugh Lines: Humorous Thoughts and Advice on How to Live Young When You're... well... Not.* Her books share her irreverent advice on marriage, hilarious how-to

lists, and her most embarrassing midlife moments. She has been featured on the Michael J. Fox Foundation website, Erma Bombeck's Writer's Workshop, *The Huffington Post*, *Scary Mommy, Midlife Boulevard, Better After 50*, and *Funny Times Magazine*. She also received a BlogHer14 "Voices of the Year" Humor award. You can find Vikki and more of her writing at laugh-lines.net.

Here's a Sneak Peek at

~~~~~~

Who Left the Cork Out of My Lunch?

By
Vikki Claflin

"At once frank and funny, edgy and heartfelt, *Who Left the Cork Out of My Lunch?* is a laugh-out-loud romp through midlife. Every woman over 40 should buy this book, and buy another for a girlfriend. Vikki Claflin is us. Pour a glass of wine, put on your Depends, and settle in with this hilarious read. Aging may suck, but Claflin makes it suck just a little less."

~Jenna McCarthy, Author
I've Still Got It...I Just Can't Remember Where I Put It:
Awkwardly True Tales from the Far Side of Forty

Big Girl Panties Society.
Rules for Membership

THE FIRST TIME I heard someone say "Put on your big girl panties and deal with it," I burst out laughing and spit my wine across my computer keyboard. My mind had an instant visual of a middle-aged woman sword fighting in nothing but her underwear. My brain goes places others' don't.

I decided then and there to start up a "Big Girl Panties Society," created to celebrate midlife women warriors.

We've been through our 20s, when anything was possible. We wanted it all, and we wanted it all at the same time. And we believed we could have it.

Through our 30s, we were focused on career climbing, finding potential soul mates, raising future world leaders, and struggling to make mortgage payments for houses we couldn't afford.

By 40, we began to come to terms with who we were and what drove us or made us happy. And we began weeding out what didn't. Many of us were on our second marriages and bearing the battle scars of divorce.

Now we're 50-something and a bit like the Velveteen Rabbit. He's a little worn, an ear lopped off, a button or two missing, and seams no longer straight, but a better bunny for his journey.

We're independent, irreverent, opinionated, and fiercely loyal to those we love. We diet if we choose to, but cheat with no apologies. Exercise activities are selected as much for their fun factor as for their ability to give us firm thighs. We've discovered that spoiling our grandchildren is easier than raising our kids. We've traded stupid stilettos for fabulous flats, and we're still hot. Sex is better than ever because we've learned what we want and we ask for it. We're happiest when we're surrounded by friends, sharing a great bottle of wine and laughing 'til our faces hurt.

If you're a woman warrior, you're in. But like any club, there are a few rules for membership.

> **You should have experienced some level of menopause.** This gives you street cred when the group conversation inevitably turns to how to deal with night sweats and fatigue. We lose patience with 30-year-old Beach Barbies claiming they'll never take drugs for menopause symptoms because it's a *natural* process. It makes us want to smack you and make notes to remind your future estrogen-popping self what a bad-ass you were at 30.

> **You should have a rudimentary knowledge of music from the 70s-80s.** At least enough to know that Kanye didn't "discover" Paul McCartney. How else will you be able to join our nostalgic, wine-induced, group karaoke during girls' night out?

> **We request that all cell phones be turned off or put on vibrate** during group meetings. This includes luncheons, spa days, wine tastings, book club gatherings, in-home retail parties, and shopping excursions. This is *our* time.

> **You must not use the word "like" more than once in any single sentence.**

➤ **No comments or quips shall be made about the group's 10 p.m. curfew**. If you want to stay and boogie-oogie-oogie (and you should know what that means) until last call, slip quietly into the women's bathroom until we've all gone home.

➤ **You must be a grandma, be pushing your offspring to make you a grandma, or at least have a grandma in your immediate peer group**. This helps us establish that you share the same historical time frame as the rest of the group. And if your boobs haven't yet fallen off their perch and migrated to your waistline, you have an unfair advantage when it comes time for our coveted, annual summer "Best Boob-Belt" award.

➤ **You cannot be offended by swearing**. We've earned it.

➤ **At any group gathering that involves food, there will be no mention of weight, calories, or diets**. We're 60. We get to eat.

➤ **There must be at least one current fashion trend in your closet that you're wearing the second time around**.

➤ **You should be able to recognize at least two elevator songs as those you dated to in your 20s**. Extra points are given if you have the original songs on your iPod.

➤ **You must be willing to view dozens of photos of grandchildren**, while listening to lengthy, detailed examples proving unequivocally that the tiny tot is obviously gifted (he can already count to 3!). Requests within the group for references on little Henry's pre-application into John's Hopkins, Class of 2032, must be honored.

➢ **You must agree to share names and contact information**, if asked, about where you got that gorgeous handbag, who cuts your hair, or who does your Botox.

➢ **No whining.** The purpose of our group is to provide support and encouragement to each other. While we're always willing to lend a shoulder and some advice (if you ask), your repeated, prolonged wailing about circumstances you have no intentions of changing will be respectfully removed from the agenda.

➢ **What is said among the group, stays in the group.** We're not in high school. Tattling or rumor-spreading about any other member will get your ass summarily booted out the door.

➢ **You must be able to laugh at yourself.** Various body parts have shifted downward like underground fault lines. Hair has stopped growing on our heads, but is now sprouting on our chins. Thighs jiggle when we're standing still. We gain weight on two Cheerios and a Diet Coke. We wear "age-appropriate" clothing. We have to record any show we want to watch that comes on after 10 p.m. We love sex, but we're usually too tired to have it. If you don't see anything funny about this, we're probably not the group for you.

I suspect that there are lots of women warriors out there. Let's find each other and celebrate. We're *fabulous*.

CRCRCR

Also From Mill Park Press

Magic Fishing Panties by **Kimberly J. Dalferes (Humor)**: A book that reminds all women of certain truths: the best pals are gal pals; all anyone needs to rule the world is a pair of black boots and a fabulous red coat; and above all else, live out loud, laugh often, and "occasionally" drink tequila.

Who Stole My Spandex? Life in the Hot Flash Lane by **Marcia Kester Doyle (Humor—Marriage & Family)**: A witty selection of stories from Doyle's madcap world of menopausal pitfalls, wardrobe malfunctions, and a family full of pranksters. No topic—no matter how crazy or unimaginable—is too taboo.

Midlife Cabernet: Life, Love, & Laughter After Fifty by **Elaine Ambrose (Humor)**: Here's proof that there is life, love, and laughter after fifty. Won the Silver Medal for Humor from the Independent Publisher Book Awards and a 4-star review from ForeWord, and ranked #1 in humor sales on Amazon. *Publishers Weekly* reviewed the book as "laugh-out-loud funny!"

Midlife Happy Hour by **Elaine Ambrose (Humor)**: Her latest kiss-my-attitude book, it explains how women can balance midlife without falling over. She invites those who have survived careers, kids, and chaos to join her for *Happy Hour*.

Made in the USA
Middletown, DE
04 June 2017